Tales2Inspire ~The Opal Collection

Stronger Today Because . . .

The Opal: A karmic stone that encourages putting out positive emotions, and teaches that what we put out comes back to us.

Dear Carol ~

Wishing you many blessings on the journey !

much Love. ♡

Adrienne

Published by *Tales2Inspire®*
tales2inspire@optimum.net

ISBN-9781703129854

Available on Amazon.com and other internet and retail outlets.

Preface

The Opal is a karmic stone, teaching us that what we put out comes back to us. From the Greek derivative "Opallios",, meaning *to see a change of color*, the opal is absorbent and reflective, helping us pick up thoughts and feelings, amplify them and return them to their source. As a symbol for the encouragement of positive emotions, this stone seems an ideal fit for a collection of stories from people who find themselves *Stronger Today Because . . .*

Each of these authors tells the story of a person or event that had an indelible impact on their life. But it takes an exceptionally skilled author to transmit such powerful emotions to their readers. These award-winning authors have accomplished this karmic task.

The stories you are about to read are all written by *Tales2Inspire* contest winners, some already accomplished authors, others about to be discovered for their special talents; some first time winners, others, repeat performers. All are welcome and equally celebrated. Following each of their stories you will find a mini biography, so you can learn about their other achievements. I am so proud of every one of them, and stand behind each author as a member of their personal cheering squad!

You might notice that once in a while I sneak in one of my own stories, simply because I love to write. It happens whenever I feel I have a story worth contributing, but rest assured, my stories go through the same anonymous vetting process as any of the other stories published in a *Tales2Inspire* collection. And often, I learn a thing or two from my fellow authors.

Lois W. Stern

CONTENTS

THE ART OF THE SOUL
by Adrienne Drake, MD

Art happens at the moment you are unseated. ~Tess Gallagher~

My dear friend, Gayla, was an enlightened individual. She was one of those rare and selfless people who truly believes in the radiance of all beings. She was skilled in her ability to help that light shine in everyone she cared for. When she became ill, I was unwavering in my optimism. I knew she was going to pull through.

Gayla had a daughter with Down Syndrome, but she did not feel sorry for herself. Instead, I believe the difficult challenges of a single mom raising a disabled daughter only strengthened her character. It made her stop and examine life's most fundamental questions: the meaning of fair and unfair, the dance of good and evil, the purpose of human suffering and the ever unfolding mystery of grace.

At the time of her diagnosis, I had known Gayla for only three years. Yet during that short time, our friendship grew into an ideal fit. Unlike my own unreachable mother, whose misfortunes and addictions left her brittle and cold, Gayla's hardships did not solidify her. Instead, they cracked her gentle heart wide open and became her greatest teachers. Gayla was only three years older than I, yet, she made me feel like a beloved daughter, as she became for me the kind of mother I had forever longed for but never had.

Gayla was an intuitive and sensitive artist. Six months before she was diagnosed with cancer, her paintings became more abstract. They became infused with dark colors and spiritual images. She painted ethereal ladies dancing by the light of the moon, and ghost riders crossing a barren desert. Once, she even painted a fallen figure, which, when the painting was turned upside down, looked to all of us in art class like an angel looking down from heaven. When we pointed that out to her, she shrugged it off with a sigh.

9

We became concerned and asked her if she were trying to tell us something. "No," she explained with a hint of sadness. "This is simply something I am going through. I'm in a sort of 'gathering in' place right now."

At that point, no one could have predicted that her paintings foreshadowed the harrowing and difficult journey that lay ahead.

After Gayla's cancer diagnosis, she maintained her positive outlook. She continued to see and reflect the goodness she saw in others. She recognized beauty in me that I never knew existed. By example and in words, she encouraged me to be the best person I could be. She helped me see and believe in my potential and my worth.

Throughout my career as a physician, I never saw anyone fight so hard to go on living. After IV chemotherapy, she took oral medications. "I will need to take these pills forever," she said. "They will keep me in remission." But her disease defied her optimism.

Gayla, home from the hospital, prepares a meal.
Barney never left her side.

Soon, she developed resistant infections. Her vertebrae thinned and fractured. She nibbled on protein bars in class. She had to force herself to eat. Despite excruciating bone pain, she agreed to participate in experimental protocols designed to treat Multiple Myeloma. She went to the City of Hope. In the brief respite she enjoyed between two grueling bone marrow transplants, she said, "I think this fatigue is the new normal, and I am not sure I like this new normal." I was crushed by this admission. It was the first and only time I ever heard her complain about her medical ordeal. A pillar of my strength was weakening. It worried me a lot.

Her paintings took on a more well-defined theme. She had always nurtured the spark of light in others. Now, she was fanning her own life force. Her painted bouquet of bronze chrysanthemums was faded, with the underside decayed to a sickly brown. Yet, you could feel its vitality as the stems and blossoms reached upward, in silent prayer, toward the sky.

The final picture she shared with us was done in broad bands of red, gold, yellow and black. Two tentative ribbons of white stood in stark contrast to those bold strokes. "This white represents hope," she explained. "Do you think I should have used a little more of it?" Off to one side, as though looking into the picture, stood a tall, dark angel ascending to heaven. This time, there was no ambiguity in the image. The tips of its toes were just lifting off the ground. This was the last day Gayla had the strength to come to class. Still, she offered to help me carry my art supplies to the car.

As her artwork predicted, her disease process was relentless. Now, haggard and exhausted, she became emaciated. She was more spirit than body, yet, drawing on some unseen force, the love in her eyes burned even brighter. She was patient. She tried to find the lessons in her suffering. Barney, her recently rescued black and tan puggle, sensed her distress. During many long hospital stays, he slept on her pillow. When she came home, he never left her side.

11

After she had failed all available treatment options, she reluctantly agreed to go on hospice. When her son, Matt, drove her home from her final doctor's appointment, they hardly spoke a word. They were completely comfortable in each other's silence.

Her memorial service was packed. Her ex-husband flew cross-country to be there. Matt, a high school music teacher, was the last to speak. He told us, through barely choked back tears, "Surely Mom and I are the lucky ones. We realized on that long drive home, that everything we needed to say had already been said. All that was left was, 'Goodbye.' "

A reception was held at Gayla's favorite restaurant. Her artwork hung on the walls. Each of us was invited to take one of her many colorful scarves neatly folded in a woven basket by the door. A looped slideshow of her life was playing. Her daughter stood in front of it. She waved to the pictures of her mother. "Goodbye, Mom," she said, as each one flashed by.

I, myself, was totally unprepared to say, "Goodbye." Why did my dear friend, such a good person, have to die? An essential prop had been pulled out from under me. I felt very, very sorry for myself. Life was so unfair.

Yet, even in death, Gayla remained a powerful teacher. In the face of her own mortality, she exhibited a quiet dignity and grace. Until the very end, she never stopped encouraging me to believe in myself. As I remembered the beauty of our friendship, I was inspired to live up to her example, and to all that she had taught me to be. I turned the hot energy of my rage, sadness and self-pity into making a collage.

The collage depicts a rugged mountain in a simple golden landscape. In the distance, gentle rain is falling from magenta clouds, hung in a peach colored sky. This ancient mountain has emerged from powerful, creative forces from deep within the earth's molten layers. I named this picture, *Tadasana*, which is the name of one of my favorite standing yoga poses. "Tadasana," in Sanskrit, means Mountain Pose. It is a grounding posture, one which promotes unwavering strength, stability and self-confidence.

Tadasana, which means Mountain Pose in Sanskrit

Gayla's final lesson to me was to transform my grief into something sustaining and supportive. Now, whenever I feel that life is unfair, I can look at my collage. Each time I do, I am revitalized. It reminds me that I didn't lose Gayla after all. Her soul lives inside that mountain, and that mountain lives in me.

ABOUT THE AUTHOR

I am a retired physician and practiced Internal Medicine and Infectious Disease as a solo private practitioner in Laguna Hills, California. I was born in Los Angeles and raised in Seal Beach, California. I went to Colorado College in Colorado Springs and graduated Magna Cum Laude with an M.A. in Mathematics. I continued my studies at Dartmouth Medical School where I received a Master of Medical Sciences before graduating with an M.D. degree from the University of Minnesota.I completed my Internal Medicine Residency and Infectious Diseases Fellowship at the Mayo Clinic in Rochester, Minnesota.

I feel blessed to have been in private practice for over twenty years. Now, I am finding many new and enriching passions. I currently teach yoga and dabble in watercolors. I enjoy spending time with my godsons, experimenting with different succulent varieties in my garden and playing with my two Snowshoe Siamese, Jingles and Bella.

Although I have published scientific articles in medical journals, I always longed to write about my experiences in training, and about some of my beloved patients whose unique lives I was privileged to witness. I wanted to tell their stories and to show the world the human side of my richly rewarding profession. Now, I will have the time.

ADRIENNE DRAKE, M.D.

EUGENE
by Rod DiGruttolo

Eugene was a big man, but his heart was even bigger. We worked together for nearly ten years and I rarely heard him utter a mean word. Oh sure, we complained about those everyday things over which we had no control; it was too hot, too cold; too wet, too dry, but Eugene always remained polite and soft-spoken and when he spoke, it was with a smile, if not on his lips, his words projected it. Our customers loved him, and many became his friends.

Ours was an old fashioned "Service Station" built on a reputation for honesty and expertise in our profession, a reputation which kept loyal customers for years. Some would often stop by, "just to shoot the breeze" as Eugene was prone to say.

Afternoon thundershowers on the West Coast of Florida are often quite severe; not only does rain come down in torrents but lightning is nearly constant, striking almost anywhere anytime. It was a hot June day, storm clouds gathered in the east rolling west toward the Gulf of Mexico. Preceding their approach, the temperature climbed into the mid-nineties and the pavement shimmered under the broiling sun. The storm would hit in about an hour, between four and four-thirty.

Shortly after three o'clock an elderly gentleman, dressed in a worn but still serviceable business suit, strolled into the shop. He asked, "Might I get a drink of water here?"

Eugene answered, "Help yerself" pointing to a drinking fountain attached to the cold drink machine.

The water was cold, and the old man drank slowly resting between sips. He stood there for nearly fifteen minutes. He'd pause between drinks, look around, and generally seemed a bit nervous.

I'd paid little heed of the man until Eugene said, "I think that old man is lost. Look, he keeps lookin' around as if he doesn't know where he is."

"Have you seen him before?" I asked.

"Not that I recall but I gotta ask if he's lost." The concern in Eugene's voice made me stop what I was doing and watch. Eugene approached him, smiling and friendly. He spoke in a soft voice that still carried the twang of his native West Virginia despite having lived in Florida for over thirty years, "Kin I help you, sir? It kind'a looks like you ain't too familiar with the area."

The old gentleman returned the smile and said, "I seemed to have lost my bearings a bit ago and don't see anything familiar. I've been wanderin' around a bit but I'm sure I'll see something I recognize soon."

Eugene cocked his head and glanced toward the sky. "Looks like a bad storm comin', best you should be inside when it hits."

"Guess you're right. Maybe you could just direct me to Kensington Park."

"Kensington Park? That's a ways off, where's your car?"

"Oh, I wasn't driving, I was walking. You see, I am staying in Kensington Park with my daughter and son-in-law. They're at work and I can't remember where either of them works." He grinned, "Don't have a phone number either."

"How'd you get here?" Eugene asked.

"Well, I decided to take a walk this morning. It wasn't so hot when I left but it sure got hot quick and I must've taken a wrong turn. I've been wandering around ever since trying to find their street, but nothing looks right."

"That's understandable. Kensington Park is about six miles north and east of here," Eugene said, "Did you walk all that way?"

"Oh my, I guess I did. I suppose that's why nothing looks right." Tears welled up in the old man's eyes.

"You know your daughter's address?" Eugene asked.

"I'm afraid I don't."

Eugene ushered the man into the business office so they could sit in the air conditioning and motioned to me. "Should I call the police?" he whispered.

I said, "Not yet, let's see what we can do." I asked the old man, "Do you have identification with you, sir?"

The old man looked at me with a vacant gaze. "I don't know, son."

"What about a wallet, do you have a wallet?" I asked.

The old man patted his suit jacket, smiled, then produced a slim wallet from his inner pocket and handed it to me. I opened the wallet. It contained two one-dollar bills, a twenty-dollar bill folded in a side pouch and numerous business cards from various businesses; but no identification.

"Do you have anything else in your pocket?" I asked. The old man patted and dug in his pockets again. This time he extracted a single sheet of notebook paper from his trouser pocket. He extended the folded paper to me and simply smiled as he sat down again. I unfolded the paper. Written on the paper in a feminine hand was a short note.

The man carrying this note is my father. His name is Phil. Please call Bonnie at 555-8866 or 555-7891 and I will come for him. Thank you.

"Phil," I said.

"That's me," the old man answered, a smile on his face.

"Your daughter named Bonnie?"

"Yep, that's her."

"Well, we're going to call Bonnie and get you home. Okay?"

"Okay," the old man said, his voice was emotionless.

Eugene shook his head. "Want me to call?" he asked. "I'm finished for the day and you still got one to go."

"Sure, but if you need help, holler."

Eugene dialed the number, all the while keeping an eye on the old man. The phone rang once and a female voice answered, a voice on the verge of panic. Eugene said, "Bonnie, your father's here and he's safe."

"Oh, thank God, you found him," she nearly shouted. I could hear her clearly and I was over six feet from the receiver. "Where is he?"

Eugene gave her the details and she said, "We were just about to call the police, but my husband wanted to make one more try at finding Dad. I don't know exactly when he'll get back, but as soon as he does, we'll pick him up."

Eugene didn't hesitate before saying, "I'll bring him home right away. He's tired and hungry."

"Bless you," Bonnie said, "He's been out since seven-thirty this morning, but we didn't know it until an hour ago. A neighbor called and we've been looking for him ever since."

Eugene took the old man home. On the way, they stopped at a drive-in restaurant and he bought his passenger a chocolate milkshake, which he devoured before he got him home. Thanks to Eugene, the old man was home before the storm hit.

Left rear: Eugene (several months before his death),
Right rear:Author, Rod DiGruttolo
Left front: Station Owner: Right front: Cashier and Owner's daughter

I learned a lot from Eugene. As an auto mechanic I learned patience, don't rush, take one step at a time; but I now realize the most important lessons came in how to deal with people. I've always had the ability to project confidence and deliver outstanding customer service in business, but showing compassion for others with troubles was not my strong suit. His slow, easy-going manner with people instilled in me an ability to look at others with compassion and empathy. To some, his slow West Virginia drawl was a sign of an uneducated man. However, I now know his studious observations were carefully weighed and decisions brilliant. He taught by example, not with a lecture, demeaning comment, or demand, but by simply being who he was.

Rest well my friend, your work on earth is done.

ABOUT THE AUTHOR

Rod DiGruttolo grew up and continues to live in Sarasota, Florida. He says, "Living in perpetual summer, adjacent to beaches and warm, clear water is as close to an ideal childhood as any boy could ask for, maybe more idyllic than life on the Big Muddy." A multiple contributor, Rod has a number of winning stories published in the *Tales2Inspire* series, including *Pappy and the Bandleader* (Sapphire Collection), *Painting a New House* (Crystal Collection), *Super Heroes* (Ruby Collection) and *Figo, the Miracle Dog* (Garnet Collection). He also has helped several authors with good stories edit them to perfection. Rod is the author of two books, **Snakes Spiders and Palmetto Bugs** and **Need to Know**, available on Amazon. He also co-chairs a writer's group in the Sarasota, Fl. area.

ROD DiGRUTTOLO

CURVES AHEAD
MJ McGrath

I was thirteen, and furiously pedaling my new green bicycle to my summer job as a mother's helper to my sister Liliane. When Liliane had suggested to my parents that they purchase me a bike for the isolated three-mile trek to her home and back, I had quickly hidden my hands behind my back and crossed every finger I could. None of the nine children, of which I was the youngest, ever had a bike bought for them before, new or used, and I got a brand new one.

Liliane lived in Glen View Heights, a '60s housing project. The front doors faced the concrete parking lot. As I approached, I had to slow down to avoid battered tricycles, push toys and energetic kids. Mothers umpired arguments from open kitchen windows. By mid-day, the sun would shine mercilessly on the quiet lot and the one abandoned dusty Ford.

I stepped into my sister's home, greeted by the sweet smell of baking, the pungent scent of a freshly lit cigarette and a neat row of children's shoes. Each right shoe had a characteristic trait, the scuff mark from a tiny foot dragged along the cement to stop the merry-go-round at the project playground. New shoes were not in the budget, but free fun was. My wage was based on my teenage palate not my pocket-book. It included bottled Cokes, the small ones, sometimes watered-down to go around, and unlimited, melt-in-your-mouth, butterscotch squares.

On that first morning, I was rewarded with more than even money could buy—the delighted shrieks of children. "Aunt Doeann is here! Aunt Doeann is here and she has a new bike!" I loved the childish pronunciation of the Jo in my name.

I hugged their tiny bodies, closed my eyes, and relished the lingering fragrance from their mandatory evening baths. I kissed their still sleepy heads while promising them a spin on my bike. Except for arms and legs, I figured each would fit in the bike's wicker basket.

Mother's helper

Being with Liliane's delightful brood of pre-school age kids, two boys—two girls, was like living in a spring garden. The energetic home life was such a change from residing with my older, staid parents. And Liliane and I often giggled hysterically. One evening, several weeks before, the baby had just been scooped out from his bath in the kitchen sink. He was laid on the counter, inadvertently by the 'catch of the day', a fresh trout someone had brought us for supper. We jokingly called the new born infant Trout, and never stopped. After all, fish and boy were 14 inches long and both wet. The trout, we had fried in a small amount of butter. Our boy Trout we had massaged with baby oil making him smell deliciously, like almonds.

Trout

That first morning, my duties included ironing children's clothing. The iron spit hot steam as I pressed tiny checkered shorts with matching cropped tops in worn-out colours of pink, mauve, and yellow. Finishing the frayed blue overalls, I carefully folded a red 'Perry Como' sweater. This 1950' style cardigan was a gift to the first-born from his grandmother. He so loved that sweater, he slept in it.

As I ironed, my mind drifted back to a few weeks ago when Liliane and I had made a cake for my father's birthday. The seven minute frosting was a challenge but we beat that icing to bits, in an old aluminum pot. We had fun. The icing turned out nice and thick but unfortunately it was also metallic grey. Out of product, out of money, out of options, we served the cake anyway.

A bright shirt, was next up to iron. However, my thoughts turned dark. The shirt belonged to my brother-in-law, Liliane's husband. He drank a lot and was always losing jobs. Oftentimes I was really frightened of him. I had heard my mother say to my sister, "Remember your marriage vows, forgive him and work hard to keep your family together". This morning, I worked hard to keep scary memories of his angry behaviours from ruining my day.

It was now lunchtime and a tray of peanut butter and jelly sandwiches filled the cheery yellow Formica table top. Liliane was upstairs and called for me. I put the five-year-old in charge and I climbed the stairs to the master bedroom.

Liliane's tone of voice reminded me of the week before when she had tried to teach me how babies were made by pointing out a pair of mating kitchen flies. Where Mother was perpetually reluctant to recognize 'womanly' milestones, my three sisters filled in, in their own time, in their own way. Liliane's approach was basic.

"Put this on," Liliane said, handing me a bra. There was nothing subtle about my sister's approach, or her mature bra size. I was just a slip of a girl and slithered easily out of my Bambi imprinted T-shirt. The bra was a bit of a "how to" puzzle.

"Clip it in the front and twist it around."

"Don't look at me!" I hollered.

Liliane's bra was more than my emerging body parts required. I poked at the nearly hollow cup and giggled. "A bit of toilet paper will fill that up," Liliane whispered. I realized the thin scratchy paper, conveniently shoved in her pocket, was in anticipation of this very thing. I stuffed it in begrudgingly as she instructed me to stand straight.

"It's a start," she said.

Bambi's image stretched tightly over my new cloth pyramids, but not without some pushback. I inspected front and side views several times that afternoon in the hall mirror and pressed and pulled as required. Liliane had spotted me and just smiled.

"Okay kids, let's have a game of 'button, button, who has the button,' before I leave. After a few games and a few kisses, I jumped proudly on my bike and started peddling home for supper. I turned back, waved to the little ones and reminded them, "We have a ride so we are going to the river tomorrow."

At the river

Peddling down the empty road, the wind warm on my face and arms, I felt energized and upright, even if my body was a little off kilter. I had had a great first day. I glanced at my new chest, pumped the pedals with extra vigour around the curves and yelled "Yahoo!" to the empty fields. All the while, my ponytail continued to chase me.

In the privacy of my bedroom, I changed into a soft, pink jersey. I smoothed my sweater over my breasts and pedal pushers. I felt like a woman when I entered the living room, late that afternoon.

My brother, in his early twenties, squinted at me and exploded into laughter. I was mortified and lowered my eyes, my cheeks searing with heat. I hesitantly met his gaze. What did he think of his little sister, with huge breasts protruding from her diminutive body? Such a large transformation since that morning.

That night at the supper table, mother could no longer deny the undeniable; my body was changing. The next day, in relative silence, she trotted me to the local Zellers department store. I fit comfortably into a 32 Double A.

Liliane could not have planned this any better.

***

I smiled a little smile for that long-ago summer of '62—a new bike, a coming of age, four precious children, and a practical big sister.

The stars had not yet aligned to help Liliane and her family. Alcoholism as a disease was not yet well recognized. Liliane had to just keep peddling, doing the best with what she had. We ate those butterscotch squares straight from the oven; we ironed faded clothing; we cherished the scent of a baby's head and we let the kids explore the river, capriciously, with rolled up pant legs and underwear showing. And yes, we stuffed a bra...

Life has unpredictable curves, sometimes fearful and sometimes dangerous. I had learned to steer these with courage, daring and where possible, with merriment, because my sister had lovingly shown me the way. It became a lifetime habit.

ABOUT THE AUTHOR

MJ McGrath was the last born of nine children (thankfully for her mother) in the small Canadian village of Apple Hill, renowned for apple orchards, but ironically no hill. Soon enough, the 'big city' beckoned MJ and a master's degree in Social Work advanced her left-leaning views which tended to get her into trouble. She believes that setting a life story down on paper is not for the faint of heart. She continues to build her childhood and adult memories with genuine stories that explore her truths, offer new understandings and lighten your heart. MJ and husband James are an adoptive family who have successfully launched their lovable son, but not without respectively turning grey and balding. MJ lives in Val des Monts, Quebec, in a lake house with her husband, their family's lovable Golden Retriever and her exotic muse, a cat who believes she can read and write.

MJ McGRATH

NEVER SAY NEVER
by Jane Vire Tichenor

As I walked down the hall toward my new classroom, I felt a sudden burst of energy and my first-day jitters vanished. My childhood dream of being a second-grade teacher was now a reality. For the next nine months, twenty-one precious children would be in my care. By using the skills I had learned in my methods classes and showing them love and compassion, they would soar like eagles. What could possibly stop me?

I soon discovered the saying "one bad apple spoils the whole bunch" was somewhat true. I had twenty angels and one fallen angel. Sammy would definitely be a challenge. I had been told by his first-grade teacher that he was a troublemaker. It didn't take long for me to understand what Mrs. Finney meant when she said, "I'm glad I don't have to put up with him anymore."

Sammy wasn't interested in anything that had to do with learning. He rarely did anything really bad in the classroom, just things such as taking pencils, knocking papers off desks, and pulling the girls' hair. As soon as they complained to me, he would smile and go back to his doodling. In fact, sometimes he was a really sweet child—when he wanted to be.

However, on the playground, he deserted his Dr. Jekyll personality and took on the characteristics of Mr. Hyde. He was like a bolt of lightning striking out at everyone in his path. If the children saw him coming, they would scatter in all directions, trying to avoid him. Whenever he caught someone off guard, chaos broke out. After each incident, he would promise to be good, but as soon as he was allowed to play again, another fight would erupt. He had been labeled *bad boy* and was living up to everyone's expectations.

I discovered his family life was unfavorable, and he had little encouragement to do better. I reached out to his parents to encourage them to become involved in helping Sammy, but they told me it was my job to teach him, not theirs. They also told me in no uncertain terms that they thought school was a waste of time because Sammy was going to work on the farm and didn't need an education.

The other teachers told me not to waste my time because he wasn't going to learn anything no matter what I tried. But my heart ached for Sammy, and I desperately wanted to prove them wrong. Where to begin? I had no idea,-but knew I had to come up with a plan to get him interested in something constructive. I agonized on how I could rechannel his negative energy into something positive. Since he obviously craved attention, I tried to think of a way to give him special attention. One thing I knew for sure - I had to make him think whatever I did was his idea since anytime I told him to do something, all he did was gripe and complain.

The wheels started turning, and before long I was ready to launch my plan. I announced to the class that I had an experiment I wanted to do but needed someone to help me. The word *experiment* was like a magic word to the students. It was difficult not to burst into laughter when they all began jumping up and down begging me to choose them. As I had hoped, Sammy was just as enthusiastic as the others and was thrilled when I chose him.

The other children wanted to know what the experiment was, but I winked at Sammy and said, "It's mine and Sammy's secret." The smile on his face said it all. He was finally excited about something. I told him we would have our secret meetings while the other students were at recess. That way none of them could spy on us and discover our experiment. Since all he did at recess was get into fights, this would help not only him but also those on recess duty.

I began by giving Sammy an oral IQ test. The results proved what I thought all along. He was a bright boy but wasn't living up to his capabilities because he lacked motivation to learn. A new approach to learning was necessary if Sammy was going to be successful.

During one of our secret meetings, I discovered he loved horses. Before our next meeting, I found some easy-to-read books about horses and placed them in the chalk tray along with the other library books I had checked out of the school library. Sammy chose one of the books about horses and asked me to read it to him. He loved the story so much that he asked me to read it to him again the next day. After reading the story, we made flash cards so he could learn all the words in the book. On Friday, he asked if he could take the book home for the weekend. My plan was working!

I was overjoyed the following Monday morning when Sammy asked if he could read the book to the class. During our meeting that day, I coached him on how to read with expression. I could hardly contain my laughter as he brought the story to life. He was a natural.

When I announced that Sammy was our reader for the day, the other students looked at each other with shocked expressions. They had never heard him read before. During reading class in first grade, Sammy sat in the back of the room and colored pictures.

As our experiment continued, I let Sammy choose his own books to read. Gradually, I incorporated the reading textbook but let him choose which stories he wanted to read. His vocabulary was growing by leaps and bounds.

Sammy also began improving in his other subjects. One day while he was taking a math test, he looked up at me and smiled. "Hey, this is easy. I got them all by myself and didn't even copy off anyone!"

I was concerned his enthusiasm for our special experiment would wear off, but as long as he was getting special attention, he was ready for our secret meetings and never mentioned missing recess. The students began to see him in a different light since he wasn't causing trouble anymore.

The day he decided he wanted to go to recess with his

classmates again, I felt a twinge of fear that he might go back to his *wild* ways, but my fear was unfounded. His classmates included him in their activities, and all was well. If anyone tried to pick on him, they would have his back.

Jane with her class of second graders

SECOND GRADE

When I first began my experiment, the other teachers shook their heads. In the hallway, they would jokingly ask, "How's 'Project Sammy' coming along?" I could hear their whispers and laughter as they headed down the hall.

I was quite apprehensive when end-of-the-year tests were to be given. I knew in my heart Sammy had made a lot of progress, but I feared facing the other teachers if he scored low on the achievement tests. When the results arrived, my hands were shaking as I opened the envelope. I took a deep breath, scanned the list for Sammy's name, and gave a sigh of relief. Sammy had scored average and above average in every subject. That's when all the laughing stopped, and Sammy was no longer labeled *bad boy*.

This experiment was time consuming and demanding, but the results were well worth my effort. I came to the conclusion that Sammy needed to feel important and have success. He longed for attention and tried to get it in the wrong way. When his needs were channeled in the right direction and achieved in a positive way, he then began to succeed.

As I continued my teaching career, Sammy was my inspiration to do everything in my power to make sure my students were successful. I was determined to never say *never* no matter how challenging the situation. Still today, anytime I am faced with a challenge, I think of Sammy and smile. Then I let my imagination run wild as I determine what course of action to take to defeat the giant in my path.

ABOUT THE AUTHOR

Jane Vire Tichenor received a B.S. from Oakland City University, an M.S. from Indiana University, and a D.E.S certification from Appalachian State University. She began her career as an elementary school teacher and continued her career as a Writing/English professor at Indiana's Community College. Professor Tichenor has received numerous awards including Oakland City University's Alumnus of the Year Award, Indiana Community College President's Award for Excellence in Teaching, and National Association for Developmental Education Award for Outstanding Service to Developmental Education Students. She has presented workshops for teachers throughout the U.S. and has written articles for several professional publications.

Since retirement, Jane has written three inspirational novels, two children's books, a book of creative ideas for English and Study Skills teachers, and several short stories.

Jane enjoys singing, writing, dancing, golfing, watching Hallmark movies, playing her ukulele and banjolele, hanging out with family and friends, and spoiling her grandsons and granddaughter.

JANE VIRE TICHENOR

THANK YOU, MISTER
By Elsa Kurt

On the morning of December 5th, 2015, I woke up and did the same first thing I always do — I checked my phone, texts, emails, then social media. As I scrolled down the stream of 'stuff,' an obituary caught my eye. There, in black against white, was a name I hadn't spoken aloud in years but thought of often. We called him Mister. He taught high school literature, poetry and photography, coached, and probably did a dozen other things I'd never realized about him. My next realization? I never said *thank you, Mister*. I'd like to honor his legacy and impact on my life with a remembrance and a thank you. It's my hope that these words drift up to whatever corner of the universe where he's holding court.

Mister was a wily, wiry, slight man. He always reminded me of what Mr. Tumnus would look like, were he human. His wire-rimmed glasses and those tufts of curly hair that sprung out like exclamations were his hallmark just as much as his customary corduroy pants, plaid shirt, and coffee in hand. Oh, and I can't forget his snarky salutations when he'd greet us at the classroom door. Those were priceless.

So many memories flood back as I write…

The many times we caught him sneaking a smoke out the window in the back of the room. He'd casually toss it out and — with only a flick of eyebrow — dare you to reprimand him. Reprimand him? *Please*, we thought he was cool. I still do. Memories: the times he'd shout and jump around in front of the room; his camera, always ready, his infectious laugh.

But my favorite memories of Mister are of the times when he'd push me to the point of tears (once) or to utter frustration (often) and even kick me out of class (once). Sounds strange, I know. Bear with me though. There was a method and a reason to the madness.

First, another confession. I was a total slacker. I drifted through school in a haze, mostly oblivious, always with this kind of passive resistance to structure and rules. Many a teacher called me ditzy, one called me a flake, and most just rolled their eyes and sent home reports that said variations of, S*he has the potential, just not the focus.* Technically, I had ADD, but that wasn't a thing then. Regardless, I rolled with the labels and cheerfully embodied them, meeting their low expectations will relish.

Elsa, High School Photo

Semester one of junior year, I passed by Mister's classroom every day to go next door for American Literature with another favorite teacher. One day, Mister — as per usual — stood in his doorway, but not with his usual funny, smirky grin, but with a serious scowl. It was directed at me.

Our one of a kind, "Mister" entertaining while educating.
Circa 1980's)

I said, *What's that look for? Whatever it is, I didn't do it!"*
Instead of laughing, he gave a 'come here now' gesture.

He said, "You know, I've looked at your records. I've
seen your IQ, and this," waving his hand at me, "*this* is a crock
of you-know-what. You're taking my class next semester."

Did he actually pull my records? Were our IQ's even in
there? No idea. Don't even care. All I know is, in that moment, I
felt... *seen*. Mister saw *me* even though I tried to hide. Before
him, almost no one took the time or the interest to call me out on
my antics and I loved it... until Mister taught me otherwise.

He saw more than what I showed, more than I knew was
under the surface. Could he have known my secret love of
words, my dreams of being a writer? The only answer is *yes*.
That my friends, is the essence of a real teacher, one who takes
the time to see more than the surface.

I enrolled in the class as ordered, making Mister my
Poetry teacher. Was that the actual name of the class? Again, I
have no idea. Poetry class consisted of reading these deep,

powerful poems — *absorb* them as he would say — and then Mister grilling us on what we thought was the underlying meaning, word by word, line by line. He was relentless, and I found it especially tortuous.

We dissected poems with fine-tooth combs, we analyzed, we speculated, we *thought*. A snowflake? Nope, it's no longer just a snowflake, it is the writer's expression of a delicate emotional connection to... ah, heck, I don't remember. But it was more than just a snowflake in a poem, trust me. We wrote poems, then broke them down for depth, meaning.

I wrote a thing — I don't recall the context — but it had to do with a horse running, and Mister prodded me to give the verse more profundity. I couldn't find the words, or in his opinion, I *wouldn't*. So, he pulled me from class, took me into an empty room, and we broke that darn verse down word by word until I pulled from some unknown well the descriptivism that gave a whole new life to a simple sentence. The horse didn't run anymore, it moved with a powerful grace, kicking up grainy clouds of white sand with sinewy flanks that pumped methodically, glistening with exertion in the hot sun.

He did that. Mister taught me the infinite power of the right words, the magical gift of making words *evoke*. Sometimes he took me there kicking and screaming, but he never quit, more importantly, he wouldn't let me quit. Mister was my first real-life hero. He certainly planted the seed that I was more than what everyone else thought I was.

I'd forgotten the impact he had on me as a writer until this little thank you note. It's been so long since I'd seen or spoken to him, but yes, my eyes are feeling an unexpected sting. I'm smiling though. The memories are flooding back and the breadth of his influence is realized.

You see, what may have seemed like madness or eccentricity, was brilliance. Mister had a gift for knowing how a student needed to be taught. For me, it was tough love and tenacity. He forced me to see more in myself, to think, to try.

He was the gardener planting seeds in my mind. Honestly? It took twenty years for those seeds to take root. But take root they did. Because of those carefully planted seeds, I'm the author of eight novels, several children's books, three novellas, two nonfiction works, and more. So, for all and much more, I say, thank you, Mister.

ABOUT THE AUTHOR

Elsa Kurt is a multi-genre author and speaker. She currently has eight novels, three novellas, a guide for aspiring writers, and several children's books published both traditionally and independently. A piece she wrote appears in the April 2019 release of Chicken Soup For the Soul: Grandparents. Her presentation, 'You Wrote It, Now What?' is now a course offering. She is a lifelong New England resident and married mother of two grown daughters. When not writing, designing, or talking her head off, she can be found gardening, hiking, kayaking, and just about anywhere outdoors. To learn more or view Elsa's work, visit https://elsakurt.com

ELSA KURT

THE SWAN
by Linda Bond

Come forth into the light of things. Let Nature be your teacher.
William Wordsworth

It's madness. Sheer madness.
I take a big breath in. A sheen of sweat is forming on my cheeks, chin, and forehead.
"Good morning," I say, while letting the all too cheery craftsmen through the door once again. Their tools and T-squares, buckets and rags, follow.
I've been living without a kitchen for two weeks.
I've eaten myself into a cookie coma, for the third night in a row.
My hair looks like its been done with a mix-master.
My House Beautiful magazines? Ripped to shreds and thrown into the cat's litter box, with the cat still in it.
It's madness. Sheer madness.
And I am not happy with how I'm handling it.

Home decorating: paint, curtains, throw cushions— a piece of cake. But being entrapped in gutted-to-the-drywall kitchen reno? My old comfortable knickers are tied in an impossible knot. And all in the name of self-closing cupboards, granite counter tops and the ubiquitous, contemporary, must-have, kitchen island. It's an "island" all right, in a sea of torture.
I swear to never again put myself through this. My working motto has gone from: do it right the first time, to—there will only be a first time.
I ask myself, *Whatever happened to that boundless primary teacher patience you once had? Has it slipped down the proverbial drain? Has it taken your perspective with it? Have you lost sight of reality?*

41

I thought I knew myself well enough to handle this, but the questions continue.

Since when did you become such an unerring perfectionist? And why? Is this a work of art you absolutely have to get right? For what purpose? For whom? Having spent months engrossed in detailed, stage-setting legwork, are you rattled to no end by spending so much hard-earned, long-saved money on something that is so obviously out of your control? Is the task simply beyond you, and you won't admit it? Has this wild disruption of your usually calm functioning life been too much?

This long-awaited project is the biggest home improvement undertaking I have ever tackled. I am ripe for over-investment on so many levels.

The lid has blown off my coping strategies.

Long ago, my husband of forty years, decided that primping our feathered nest was way outside any interests of his. However, he supports my efforts by taking his steadfast role as battered spirit booster to heart.

He tells his workout buddies, "Linda handles the renovations. I handle Linda."

Even that isn't working.

This frazzled demeanour is not the way I usually am, nor the way I want to be.

While struggling to make sense of it, the frenzy continues.

The comely young electrician arrives to finish up the well-planned "layers of lighting". I closet myself in the back room, again. Before long, he knocks on the door. He holds a rag to his temple.

"There is something I have to show you," he says slowly. "I slipped and hit the light fixture, but it didn't break," he adds quickly. His face winces. "I'm afraid my screwdriver left a gouge in the cabinet by the sink."

The rag, now blood red, is covering a corresponding gouge in his forehead.

"Oh my! Are you sure you're okay?"

"I'm fine," he assures. "This hurts you more than it hurts me."

Later that week, the cabinet maker returns with filler and touch-up paint.

"You know what they say," he consoles. "It's the flaw that makes it perfect."

The Renovations 101 Manual forgot to mention that.

So why do you even stay home during all these shenanigans?

Another question, this time with several answers.

Are you kidding?

Nobody wants to hear how your modern, custom-made, cream-coloured cabinetry arrived glazed with an unexpected antique brown finish.

Or, how your carefully chosen slab of granite, clearly marked "ON HOLD", got sold to somebody else.

Or, that on the one day you did decide to leave town, your back splash was installed in an unforeseen slapdash-where's-the-cash manner.

Or, that it took no less than three re-orders to get your shiny new microwave right.

But wait, there's more.

Sigh.

Written in the dust on the coffee table is the word —"HELP!"

***

The morning comes when I take my fourth mug of extra strong coffee, and my five-star headache out onto the balcony—the far end of the balcony. I sit in my calmest repose:

back straight, teeth clenched. I survey the familiar waterfront scene that, for some time now, has been ignored. Having decided to give reading a go, I resort to a steamy Jackie Collins novel. My eyes drop.

Barely moments later, I look up again.

Just below, there is a singular, pearl-white swan.

The serene image bobs with a rhythmic cadence as it reflects perfectly in the tranquil waters upon which it rests.

The Swan – the Teacher

She stretches her long neck toward the sun, then dips it into the cool water, and brings it up again.

She drifts with poise, and lightness.

The ripples around her wave gently outward.

I am mesmerized.

My jaw slackens as my neck rolls from side to side.

My body relaxes into the chair.

My feet drift up to rest upon a footstool.

My face turns toward the sun . . .

Like a flower reopening its petals with the rising light of

day, I go inside, roll on some lipstick, and slip out the front door.

Along the peaceful shore my walking eases into a rhythmic cadence.

My breathing keeps pace. The air is fresh, and clear. There is a paddling of ducks cavorting merrily within a marshy alcove.

A smile comes across my face.

A heron stands upon the bank. Watching. Contemplating.

I watch, and contemplate.

It is only a kitchen, my dear. There is a whole other world out there, floating by, that you are not even seeing. You know that life itself is a multi-faceted project. Some parts are easy. Some not. So don't let troubles take away your smile. Rise above the chaos. Savour this beautiful morn. Take heed.

After more restorative walks, I feel my inner swan resurfacing. I find new resolve to feed and nurture her. And stay the way. Today. Tomorrow . . .

***

Finally, the kitchen gets done, with smiles all round. I have come to love the glazed cabinetry, flaw and all. It's fun demonstrating "the light show", even if it did cost an arm and a leg, and a forehead.

The kitchen might be finished—but I'm not finished—with myself.

I need more time.

I keep the story of the swan sheltered within my soul.

Not long after, an unexpected gift appears outside my door. A note reveals that an old friend has left it while passing by.

It reads, "This is from my collection. I want you to have it. It reminds me of you. Within the box there is a singular, sparkling, crystal swan, small enough to fit in the palm of my hand, as if resting on tranquil waters.

The Gift of Inspiration

In the years that follow, I remain humbled by the enduring lessons that ripple through my days:

Honour and protect the harmony of a calm life. Never take it for granted.

Be content to slip through time with the quiet grace of a swan.

ABOUT THE AUTHOR

LINDA BOND writes out of the box and into your life. Her personal stories leave you with chuckles, images, and insights that call to mind memories of your own. Her 1960s teenage tale, *Forbidden Love,* is a contest winner. With a "writers helping writers" philosophy, she leads workshops with spirit and creativity. She coaches others so their stories of a lifetime can be preserved and shared. She celebrates a finished piece by making her husband of fifty years a world-class martini. Linda and Martin live and sail on the Bay of Quinte, Belleville, Ontario.

LINDA BOND

ADAM
by Nancy Perry

He looked like a typical 12 year old boy – hands and feet too big for his body, shirt still tucked in because he hasn't had a chance yet to squirm and stretch and move his body within the confines of the combination desk and chair. He met my car every morning and we exchanged small talk as I walked toward my office – how's math going? Did you finish your essay? It is not unusual for a student to latch on to a favored adult in the school so I thought nothing of it.

Then one morning he said "I wish you were my mother." The number one rule in school counseling is never to say anything bad about a child's parents so I made some flip remark about my being on my good behavior at school. "I bet you don't try to hurt your children," he replied. The antennae went up and I suggested that we needed to have a little talk in my office.

He told me that his mother had recently remarried and had a baby and didn't want him any more. I talked about the stress of a new baby and how it would eventually pass and his mother would be her old self again. "If I live that long," he said. He then related a story of his mother chasing him with a heavy glass coke bottle, trying to hit him in the head. "We'll talk more about this later," I assured him. As a school counselor, I was required to report any kind of abuse. Was this abuse or just a stressed mother and a sassy kid? I decided to call Child Protective Services and let them decide.

To my surprise, there was an open file on Adam, beginning when he was two years old. His mother had lit matches under his fingernails to "teach him not to play with fire." "We'll investigate," the caseworker said. A couple of weeks later I got a call confirming what Adam had told me. "However," said the caseworker, "Adam is old enough to get out of his mother's way so he should stay in the home – and we'll keep a check on his mother."

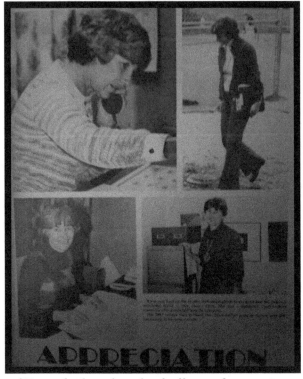

Photos of Nancy both in the school office and as tennis coach (top right)

Adam and I worked out some strategies he might use to avoid conflict and all seemed to be going well. Then one afternoon, after school was out and the halls were vacant, Adam showed up in my office. "I've come to say good-bye," he said. There go the antennae again.

"What do you mean 'good-bye'?" I asked.

"I'm running away. I can't take it any more."

"Now, Adam, that will only make things worse. Your mother will call the police to find you and you'll be in even deeper trouble," I said.

"She doesn't care," he replied. "Call her and find out for yourself." He handed me the phone. I prayed she wouldn't answer but she did.

"Mrs. Campbell, Adam is in my office and he says he is going to run away. I told him you would really be upset."

"Good riddance," was the reply and the telephone went dead.

"I guess we go to Plan B," I said. Of course the caseworker was unavailable but they would look into it in the morning. Frustration! My right brain said, "Take him home and envelop him in the warmth of the family." My left brain sprouted red flags and shouted "Legal problems!" Reason won out. "Why don't Adam and I come sit in your office until someone can help him," I said. That did it. They told me that someone would be out to get him as soon as possible. His caseworker arrived and I assured Adam that he would be safe and that I would be in touch with him.

The next day I went to the temporary shelter where he was to stay until a more permanent arrangement could be made and we talked about his future and what he could become.

Then one day, Adam disappeared from my life – moved to a group home in another city. I heard through the grapevine that he had gotten in trouble with the law and had been sent to the euphemistically called Boys Training Center. I felt terrible. Was it a mistake to file a report? Could we have worked something out until he was old enough to be on his own? It was a lesson learned – at Adam's expense.

Fast forward – Thanksgiving, eight years later. My husband and I had just returned from a lovely dinner at my daughter's home. I was feeling warm in the glow of family love. I noticed a message on the answering machine. It was Adam – please call. I hesitated. I did what I thought was right at the time and it didn't work out. What now? Do I really want to get involved again? But of course I had to return his call and tell him I was sorry.

"What a surprise, Adam. It's been so long."

"Yes, eight years," he said. "I am married to a lovely lady who has two children so I am a father."

"Wonderful, Adam. What are you doing?"

He told me that he was going to the university and that his English teacher was encouraging him to write a book about his life. "You're in it," he said.

"Is that good news or bad news?" I quipped. We chatted a while until I couldn't stand it anymore. "Why did you call me today, Adam?"

"We were sitting around our Thanksgiving table and each of us was saying what we are thankful for. When it was my time, without thinking, I said I was thankful for you. I've made some bad decisions but I always knew that you believed in me and that I could have a good life. You gave me a reason to live. I wanted to say thank-you."

That day, as I bathed in the warmth of my conversation with Adam, I wrote myself a letter.

Dear Nancy,

I know you are burdened by the fear of making decisions that could adversely affect the lives of others. You are not God. You can only decide based on the best information available to you. Stop beating yourself up. Do what you think is right and let the chips fall where they may.

Your Alter-Ego

ABOUT THE AUTHOR

I am a Texan by birth but have spent most of my life in Maine – wintering in Florida after retirement. I have professionally been in education in several capacities – classroom teacher, school counselor, Maine Department of Education consultant in school counseling, career development consultant in a federal agency and executive director of the American School Counselor Association. Although I have been published extensively on educational topics, after retirement I decided to fulfill my long-held desire to write children's books. I have two published books, *Duffy the Lonely Dragon* and *Don't Call Me Baby*. I am married with four ordinary children and eight incredible grandchildren.

NANCY PERRY

TRIUMPH AFTER TRAUMA
by Maria Jordan

On a balmy Wednesday morning in June, 1999, I had a spring to my step starting my day as Nursing Director at the largest State Hospital in Pennsylvania. I loved my work. I loved my home. I loved life in general.

Don't get me wrong, my responsibilities could wear me out physically and mentally. Some nights my feet felt like I had climbed Mount Everest on roller skates. Some days my head felt like it would explode if stuffed with one more detail.

Overall though, I felt like I was at the top of my game – strong, centered and purposeful in life. I prided myself on excellent organizational and time-management skills.

I kept physically strong by walking most days and dancing with my energetic black Labrador Retriever, Alvin. My hobbies of needle work and solving logic puzzles kept my mind active, focused and peaceful.

On the job, I was a master juggler of 650 nursing staff and the 650 patients under my care.

* David Connors was a 40 - year old, male nurse who had been employed at the hospital for about ten years. When I met him in 1990, I noticed his demeanor was suspicious about people and things in general. He was trusting and open with me, not perceiving me as a threat. Yet I felt on edge in his presence and avoided contact whenever possible in the beginning years.

Later, as Nursing Director, I didn't have the luxury of ignoring staff concerns about Connors. Countless hours were spent addressing his unsafe practice and erratic behaviors. I was able to finally terminate him in April, 1999 for drug impairment and unsafe nursing practice.

I dreaded any contact with him, whether at a scheduled meeting or the many times he burst into my office unannounced irrational, threatening and thankfully always cut short by a protective staff person. I felt giddy and safe upon his termination – free at last from his unsettling presence.

Then, on this sunny June day, David Connors burst into my office. The same man who creeped me out with his mere presence was now brandishing a gun inches from my face. I wanted to both collapse and run out of the room. Neither option was possible as he forced me to lock the door and hand over my keys.

Waving me away from the door with his gun, he began to rant about "the conspiracy theory", wanting me "to come clean about it". He demanded the presence of the state governor, the town mayor and other county officials. As I tried to comprehend his rambling, I watched in horror and disbelief as he fired four successive shots around my body. The first shot grazed my left wrist, while the second lodged in my right wrist. He next penetrated my shoe, specifically my fifth, right toe and he finished with a bullet in my left breast.

In less than a heartbeat, pain seared through every fiber of my body like a wildfire. The sound of gunshots and my own blood curdling screams filled the room. I was propelled back into my chair, collapsing in a heap. The sight of bright red blood melting into my lime green blouse convinced me I was going to die.

Over the hours, my body physically weakened as I was forced to change positions, move away from the windows and assist Connors in retrieving sandwiches, juice and cigarettes from the hallway.

I tried my best to keep my mind and thought processes strong. I often stared at the looming clock on my office wall. This ugly clock grounded me, giving me food for thought when nothing else was in my control. At night, I would not allow myself to sleep. I wanted to be present and alert if these were to be my final hours on Earth.

I didn't speak over these hours, as I didn't want to further provoke Connors. My mind, however, was going a mile a minute.

I conjured images of the many strong women in my life, both alive and dead. I imagined their words of empowerment, support and love. This mental diversion allowed me to block my physical agony somewhat.

I thought about when my first boss called me to the office for being two minutes late. It didn't matter that I drove in a torrential downpour with flooded roads and was usually compulsively early. Sixteen years later, I wondered if I would have been likewise counseled if my excuse for lateness was "being held hostage".

As time passed, I thought of meetings and rounds I had missed. On Thursday, I remembered that I had scheduled a vacation day to take my Mother to a doctor's appointment and lunch. Thursday night I had planned to swing by work to attend a retirement gathering for a nurse colleague.

Priorities that had been at the top of my To-Do List hit rock bottom as I worked to keep my focus and determination on survival. My entire mindset shifted to a minute-by-minute game plan.

From start to finish, the nightmare of being held hostage lasted forty-six hours. This translates to 2,760 minutes. Believe me, I was counting.

Then, on Friday morning, the 46th hour, the State Police sent an explosive through my office window. Rattled, Connors shot me two more times in my abdomen. These bullets travelled through to my spine. Falling to the floor, I looked up to a SWAT team standing over me. Voices screamed: "Go, go – let's get out of here". In seconds, I was lying on a stretcher, being quickly transported down some steps and out the door into the brightest and warmest sun ever. I gulped in all the fresh air my lungs could handle, staring into the kind and compassionate eyes of my flight nurse angels. I was weak but convinced that I would live. I was finally safe.

Recovery was a long and slow process. The toughest part was dealing with my physical limitations gracefully.

57

I was a nurse who was not patient being a patient. The former me hiked an average of twenty miles a week. The recovering me hobbled a few steps before collapsing in exhaustion, pain and frustration. My intricate and precise cross stitch projects were placed on hold, replaced with simple, one-step craft activities in Occupational Therapy.

After my discharge from the hospital and physical rehabilitation, Alvin intuitively knew our dancing days were over. He was, however, my constant companion during the recovery process. A couple of years later a yellow Labrador Retriever puppy, Aunt Baby, joined our home – bringing her own special brand of unconditional love and acceptance.

Alvin and Aunt Baby

In 2004, I began working as a nursing professor at a local university. I felt drawn to this role in education – one where I could positively influence and shape the thinking of my profession's future. With this professional decision, I began to feel triumphant over the trauma of 1999.

Now I assist future nurses with their clinical rotations in behavioral and community health nursing. I share my experience, stressing the importance of safety in the workplace and following one's instincts, with each of my students.

This incident has taught me that vulnerability is the foundation of my strength. It's alright, even necessary at times, to ask for and to receive help. Healing became possible once I accepted my temporary physical and emotional limitations. I learned to acknowledge and work through feelings of anger, frustration and embarrassment. Twenty years later, I know that time is the greatest healer.

By all counts, I should have died twenty years ago. It is a blessing to be alive and kicking. I know first-hand that tomorrow is not promised. I am ever grateful for today. Out of this horrendous experience came a resolve to appreciate and embrace my intuition, self-awareness and *inner* strength.

* This is an accurate memoir of my life story, though I have changed the name of the perpetrator to David Connors.

ABOUT THE AUTHOR

Maria Jordan lives near historic Valley Forge, in Montgomery County, Pennsylvania with her husband and two dogs. Throughout a thirty five year nursing career, she has served a number of clinical, consultative and administrative roles in the field of Mental Health and Community Nursing. Maria currently works as a professor in a local university where she has developed a course on "Safety and Recognizing the Signs of Potential Workplace Violence".

Check out more of Maria's books and writing at:

www.marcoujor.com

MARIA JORDAN

MR. HOOTS AND ME
by Rodney Stotts

A falconer: A person who hunts with birds of prey

As a youngster, I lived in a gritty neighborhood in southeast Washington D.C. I had few positive role models to follow from those surroundings. My dad was murdered when I was sixteen years old. You know, It's bad enough to lose a parent who has become sick and died, but at least then you get some support and sympathy from others. But no one felt sorry for me about my dad's death. He had been murdered by one of his girlfriends, who became so enraged after one of his beatings that she poisoned him.

As for my mom, even though she was addicted to crack, she was a good mom. Somehow she always managed to be there for me, my older brother and two sisters. No matter what she was going through, she made sure that we were all taken care of. There were times when she didn't eat so we could eat. She made sure we all had clean clothes even if she dressed in rags. But mostly it was the values that she instilled in us: honesty, love, commitment and trust, that probably saved us from the streets.

When I was ready to go out on my own, I needed to prove I had an income in order to get an apartment. I went to a job fair where I learned about a small nonprofit called the Earth Conservation Corps. I began to work for them, earning a $100 weekly stipend. It was our job to clean trash from Lower Beaverdam Creek, a polluted waterway of the Anacostia River. Little by little, I could see that the river was beginning to recover. Heron, osprey, beaver and other wildlife were returning to this once junk-filled tributary.

I even helped the U.S. Fish and Wildlife Service and the National Arboretum return Bald Eagles to our river. They brought eagle chicks from Wisconsin to the Anacostia, where they had once thrived, but gradually disappeared because of the pollution in the river. For four years, we took four baby eaglets each year, put them in a hatch box and hoisted it 130 feet up into a tree. We fed them using that same hoist system, so they would not rely on human intervention for their food. We knew it was important for these eaglets to remain wild, so that at the end of the year they could be released and returned to the Anacostia.

The Earth Conservation Corps started a program to educate people on the importance of raptors, birds of prey, including hawks, eagles, vultures, kites, ospreys, falcons, and owls. These birds are higher than any others on the food chain, so they serve an important role in helping to keep our environment clean. One day a non-releasable owl named Mr. Hoots was introduced into the program. I remember that day in 1998 as if it were yesterday. I was standing there, this slender black guy from the ghetto, with a Eurasian eagle-owl on my arm, a bird that seemed as big as a dog to me. I felt every range of emotion you can possibly imagine: excitement, fear, love, anxiety . . . and then, when I put that owl down, I felt empty. Somehow I sensed that this eagle was about to change my life.

Once I recognized that feeling in me, I thought about the powerful allure of birds of prey. It was a magical feeling, hard to put into words, but I knew I wanted to spread that same feeling to others.

Rodney with Mr. Hoots, down in McPherson Square

I thought about reaching out to youngsters who, like me as a kid, needed a new path. I was aware that every day young people in the city were dying senseless deaths, and knew that would continue unless someone stepped in to help them. It seemed the same with the raptors. If we didn't trap the juveniles to help them mature as independent beings, the vast majority wouldn't make it to adulthood. I began to put it together in my head. I felt ready to do something to inspire these youngsters, just as Mr. Hoots had inspired me.

Today I have a focus and a purpose. I am a licensed falconer, working as director of raptor conservation and youth empowerment at the nonprofit Wings Over America.

I am also the raptor program coordinator for Earth Conservation Corps. I visit about fifty schools in the D.C. area each year where I introduce children to several raptors up close and personal, giving them a chance to interact with these magnificent birds. And Mr. Hoots, the male eagle-owl that changed my life, accompanies me to all these programs. He vocalizes loudly. Sometimes I toss him food, which he catches in his talons, much to the delight of his young audience. But it's the enormous size of this raptor that amazes everyone the most.

Lola, Rod's first Eurasian eagle owl

I also work with teens through partnerships with the Metro Police Department, the Department of Youth Rehabilitation Services and Youth Challenge Academy. In addition, I started RodneysRaptors on the grounds of the city's New Beginnings Youth Development Center, where Wings Over America is based. Through this program, young people learn to care for, handle and feed the raptors. They help build aviaries for the birds too. Although at first they often don't recognize the new skills they are learning, a lightbulb goes off when they realize they have just mastered a useful carpentry, plumbing or electrical skill. It gives me immense pleasure when I see this transformation on the faces of youngsters immersed in these nature programs.

Rodney and Agnes, a Harris Hawk (named after the woman who wrote the stories for One Life to Live and All My Children)

Am I stronger today? You bet! I am a man who has turned a once bleak life into a life of purpose, all channeled through that owl named Mr. Hoots, the owl who helped me turn my life around.

ABOUT THE AUTHOR

I am not an author, but felt my story is one that should be told because I want to give others hope. *Learning to Fly*, a book about my story, is currently under consideration for publication as well as a soon-to-be-released documentary titled *Sanctuary.*
I am so proud to be one of the few African-American falconers in the USA. My passions are my family, my five beautiful children and all animals large and small.
I feel a deep sense of satisfaction that before my mom left this earth, I not only made her proud of me, but also proud of the things I am doing,

RODNEY STOTTS
(with two of his grandchildren)

VOICES THAT MATTER
By Vanya Erickson

It never ceases to amaze me what my third-grade students have been exposed to. Every day I'm compelled to respond to their worries. "Where do homeless children eat?" "Why do companies destroy rainforests to mine tungsten, just so phones can vibrate?" "Dad insists I go to Stanford when I grow up. What if I don't get in?"

Lord have mercy. What happened to childhood? When I first started teaching twenty-five years ago, these topics never came up. My students' concerns were neatly contained: friends being mean; a brother leaving for college; a pet dying. Now, my students' voices shake with anger and confusion.

This was a perfect teachable moment! I'd have my students write and perform TED Talks. The next day, I introduced the idea by showing them TED Talks given by children from all walks of life: Malala Yousafzai who received the Nobel Peace Prize after being shot in the face for daring to go to school; a brilliant twelve-year-old app designer who began inventing at the age of eight; a teenager with Progeria, who eloquently shared the difficulties of living with premature aging. When we finished watching, the kids discussed the powerful messages.

The next day, I told them, "Today is momentous because you are going to have the opportunity to do something I've never done before. You are going to write a TED talk. Grab your notebooks and start a list of things you feel strongly about." There was a lot of chatter as they got to work, ideas pouring onto the page.

My mind whirled. Would all of them land on a topic and stick with it? Would they be able to support their idea and sustain a four-minute speech in front of an audience? Was I crazy for asking them to do this?

As the days passed, they went deeper, falling in love with their ideas. When they needed help, we conferred at my little round table. I fielded a cauldron of questions: "What if what I want to say will upset my mom?" "Can I write about something positive?" "What do you call it when someone says you can't do something because you're a girl?"

One boy who rarely engaged, waited until others weren't around before approaching me. He looked at the floor and whispered, "May I write about finding happiness with my new Labrador retriever?" I beamed and said yes.

When it was time to practice, I introduced the importance of body language, explaining that showing your palms helps to gain the trust of your audience. They seamlessly incorporated gestures into their speeches.

Soon they presented to partners, then small groups, finally writing key thoughts on notecards for their presentations. And you know what? Every single student completed this task— even those who had never finished a writing assignment before.

The students were going to perform for their parents and administrators. I wanted a full house – for the classroom to be packed with parents loving their children. So, I wrote newsletters and reminders and asked all students to dress up – because when we do, it tells the world we're doing something important. I spent hours making sure the official program was perfect. I bribed the custodian with my favorite wolf mug he'd often admired so he'd vacuum my classroom the night before.

We scheduled our TED performance first thing on a Friday. The night before I decorated the classroom with maroon curtains I miraculously found on sale. I covered my whiteboard —the stage backdrop—with black butcher paper and painted a bright TED TALKS! sign on it. Then I dragged all desks out of the way and arranged their chairs theater-style, to accommodate the audience.

TED Talks

The next morning, the children gasped as they filed into the classroom. They moved like royalty in their satin and velvet, their neckties and hats. "Circle up!" I called when we heard parents in the hallway. The students moved their bodies into a well-practiced huddle. Would this all go as I hoped?

I scanned each of their faces. "I am so very proud of you. It's been an honor working with you. Your speeches are powerful." I smiled. "Breathe…take your places and break a leg!" I opened the door to a crowd of adults.

One by one, these bright eight and nine-year-olds shared thoughts and fears, some personal and others global: the realization that skin color seems to dictate who has power; the outrage they felt learning that not everyone has access to health care; the joy of teamwork while playing hockey. One boy farted as he stood to speak; his consuming laughter melting all of us.

Then as calmly as if he had just said good morning, he stood and delivered a jaw-dropping speech on ocean pollution and how to stop it.

This was followed by a passionate speech by a young girl who spoke of rushed dinners in the family van in between Chinese school, violin, swimming lessons, Tai-Kwon do, math and writing tutors—and the desire to do the things she loved.

Finally, the littlest boy, the one who at every recess stood on the edge of the playground and watched others, padded over and took the stage, his dark hair falling into his eyes. I swallowed hard, clutching a tissue. I knew what he was about to say.

"I'm here today to talk about loneliness, something I know a lot about." His voice was so soft the audience leaned forward in their seats, their eyes riveted to his face. "Ever since I moved here, I have hoped to make a friend, but nobody seems to notice me." A woman sniffed as I watched several students, their mouths agape, listening to their classmate's speech. But this boy was a problem solver. He only wanted a friend. He explained that he had convinced his mom to get a dog, so he'd have a pal. Her saying yes was a life changer. His was the speech about finding happiness. I wanted to leap from my seat and hug him.

As the audience erupted into applause, the woman seated next to me in the back row leaned over and whispered, "May I please have the contact information for this boy? I'd like to set up a play date." I nodded and squeezed her hand.

He had done it. They had all done it, their euphoria palpable as the students strutted around the classroom, their parents rushing to hug them. I stood and marveled. Here I was at the end of my final year of teaching, with just twenty-six days left before I retire, and I had done what others said was impossible. My students were no longer frightened to speak. They were eager to change the world through their voices.

But I wonder if my students know how deeply they've inspired me. Their words have restored my hope for our planet;

their sense of fairness has compelled me to rise up and speak out; they've demonstrated that laughter is an antidote to high-stakes testing. In a nutshell, it's because of my students that I do what I do. Their curiosity, passion, and dedication has seamlessly transformed me from a by-the-book teacher to a creative mentor. Awesome work!

ABOUT THE AUTHOR

Vanya is the award-winning author of *Boot Language*. She's
spent decades teaching writing as well as mentoring educators in
the oldest, continuously used schoolhouse in California. Her
essays have appeared in a dozen literary journals and
anthologies. Find out more about Vanya at
www.vanyaerickson.com.
2019 WINNER: Indie Book Award (Overcoming Adversity/
Tragedy)
2019 SILVER: Benjamin Franklin Award (best new voice)
2019 SILVER Readers' Favorites Award (Memoir)
2019 FINALIST Indie Excellence Award (Memoir as well as
Regional Nonfiction: The West)
2019 FINALIST International Book Awards (Narrative
Nonfiction)

VANYA ERICKSON

WHAT IS LIFE?
by Melissa Noel

Life is a journey. Life is a race. Life is a highway to heaven. Some people say life is what you make of it. I am going to tell you a thing or two about life. Throughout my lifetime I have been used and abused. I've been called all kinds of names. I've been robbed of my womanhood and have been cheated of being a mother. Maybe I would have been a great mother, the best mother that I could be.

Life, what is life? Where does life begin? I will tell you. My life began in my mother's womb. We each are given different gifts: Eyes to see with, ears to hear with. I think I was given the gift of perception - the gift to sense some things that happened to me, maybe even before I was born. I seem to remember my mother crying out while I was still in the womb, saying that my father was dead. But maybe these are just words I heard as a tiny child, I can't say for sure. But one thing I do know for sure is that when I heard those cries, I recognized the fear in her trembling voice: What would she do with me when I entered this cold world? Where would I sleep? What would I eat?

I have so many early memories, but most of all, I remember my mom always praying. She prayed that God would take this new life and bless it. Mummy used to say, "Father, this life in my belly is yours." The last day she said that was April 14, 1986, the day I was born. It was around Easter time - well, during Good Friday to be exact. At 5:15 p.m. a new life entered this world at ten pounds and five ounces.

I lived with my grandparents, my mother and my uncle. I always thought that my father was dead, until one day when I was three years old, I saw him. My whole body stiffened. It was like eating ice cream on a cold day. I felt numb, frozen inside and out, devoid of emotion of any kind. I didn't know what to do. And then it came to me. I prayed. At the age of three, I prayed to my father to help me be the best daughter in this lifetime.

Well I grew up without him in my life, but I was the best daughter that my mother could ask for.

At the age of eleven, I knew how to pray well. I was smart and doing well in school. I had my grandparents at my side. I loved going to church with them. Somehow I felt life wasn't meant to be this good. I was right. I was watching television one day after school when my uncle came and did things to me that no man should do to a child. After he was finished, I cried and cried. I had no way of knowing that his abuse would continue and keep me crying for years. I asked myself, "What is life?" But I got no answer. I prayed for God to help me to be strong and to stand up for myself. Despite my tears and prayers, his abuse continued for years. I was sure this was the worst thing that could ever happen to me in this lifetime. I was wrong.

My grandmother had always been like a second mother to me. One afternoon, I came home and discovered that she was in the hospital. Granny died months after. I thought the pain I endured from my uncle's abuse was the worst burden a girl can bare, until I lost my grandmother. I never thought I would recover. My mother compounded those moments when she decided to send me to the United States. Still grieving, I left my other best friends, my grandpa, and my mom behind.

It was tough, but somehow I remained strong enough to handle it. That day was bittersweet: sweet because one of my prayers was answered - my uncle would never touch me again — bitter because I was leaving my papa behind. For some reason I knew that I would never see him again. I was right. He died when I was fourteen years old. I thought to myself, "What is life?" But I got no answer.

At the tender age of sixteen, I found myself pregnant. I was happy, but also sad, because I didn't know how to tell my mother. How could I tell her that her baby was having a baby? I didn't know what to do because maybe this was the time to start my family right. I built up the courage to tell my mother and the next day I was at the clinic. That was the worst day of my life. I lost a big part of me that nobody could replace. For years I carried this buried within me. I didn't get to finish school. I dropped out. I didn't know what to do with this thing called life. But I remembered to pray. I prayed for forgiveness for what I'd done, prayed that when the time was right, to help me be the best I can be.

At the age of twenty-one, I met my best friend, Arionne. She is like the sister I never had. She taught me a thing or two about life, showing me that life is a lesson you have to learn so when trouble comes your way, you can handle it. To be truthful with you, I think life is like a bowl of soup. When you're sick, you've got to eat all of your vegetables, even though you don't like them, because it makes you stronger. I know I am stronger today because of all the vegetables that I have had to swallow in my lifetime. Without them, I may not have been able to get through this thing called life.

Footnote: When a retired teacher by the name of Michael Imhof entered Melissa's life, he recognized special strivings in this young woman and offered to teach her English without charge. He explains: "Melissa is undocumented. She strives to get her GED. I teach her English gratis. When Melissa gave me a hint of her story, we found a tale full of heartbreak and hope. This is the first competition she has entered."

Melissa with her friend, Tamara and Mr. Imhof

ABOUT THE AUTHOR

My name is Melissa. I am a twenty-five year old black woman from the Caribbean. I am courageous, intelligent and hard working. I have been faced with incredible hardships which have taught me the arts of courage, perseverance, hope and faith. I invite you to discover extremely personal revelations about myself and my life.

MELISSA NOEL

LOST IN PINK
by Janet Rice

He hangs his legs over the side of the bed, turns to look at his wife sleeping peacefully beside him, and places his head in his hands. A prayer catches in his throat. The remarks of the neurologist weigh heavy on his mind: "progressive dementia, poor judgement, problems recalling words and speaking, changes in personality…" Like her mother before her, my mom has Early Onset Alzheimer's Disease. She is only 50 years old.

Rising from their bed, Dad puts on his flannel robe and slippers and goes to the kitchen to start the coffee percolating. He showers, shaves and dresses in his business suit and blue striped tie. Then, he walks to his wife's side and softly touches her shoulder. "Honey, it's time to get up." She looks at him, confused. "We're going into New York City today. The bank is giving me a gold watch. Come. I have breakfast waiting. Let me help you get dressed."

Dad

Obedient, she gets up and takes his hand. He puts on her deodorant, bra and underpants. Then, he carefully slips her pink polyester dress over her head. It is the one she always wore for special occasions. He puts on her knee high stockings and patent leather shoes, then walks her to the dressing table. She takes the hair bush and stares at the face in the mirror while she tentatively combs her thick black hair. An unfamiliar face stares back.

They drive to the Jamaica train station to take the subway into the City. The platform is crowded with impatient people and she is frightened. Dad places his arm around Mom's shoulder and guides her through the throngs to a seat on the train, then stands like a shield in front of her. His hand grips a pole to his right. Comforted, she leans back in her seat, looks around the train, and then at him.

After thirty minutes, they get off the subway and walk three blocks to the main building of New York City's library system on the corner of 42nd St. and 5th Ave. He notices the two majestic stone lions, named Patience and Fortitude, who stand guard at the bottom of the stairs.

Taking Mom's hand, Dad leads her up the steps and through the halls to the Rose Reading Room. It is the size of a football field and holds forty-two white oak tables with sixteen seats at each table. The marble floor announces every step as they walk halfway down the room. They stop at a table where there is only one young woman reading. He sits his wife down at the far side of the table and places a newspaper in front of her. Turning her head to look at him, he whispers, "Now remember, you must stay here and wait for me. I have to go pick something up. I'll be back soon." He looks her right in the eye and holds her chin. "Promise me you will stay here. Don't move."

She says nothing and looks at the newspaper. He quickly heads to the exit, glancing back at his wife. He runs down 5th Ave. to the Park Ave. branch of his bank and takes the express elevator to the conference room on the 41st floor. Stopping to catch his breath, he adjusts his tie and enters the room filled with his immediate supervisors. While his boss gives a heartfelt speech, honoring his thirty years of service to the bank, Dad watches the clock.

None of his co-workers knew of Mom's illness. After warm handshakes and brief good-byes, he reverses his course and races back to the library.

When Dad gets to the room where he left his wife, the newspaper lies untouched. She is gone. Frantically, he looks around. The tables are now filled with people. He asks if anyone has seen a woman in a pink dress. Someone says, "She left ten minutes ago." He walks up and down the long hall and stops outside the ladies room. When a woman comes out, he asks about a lady in a pink dress. She gives him a strange look and hurries past.

His heart is pounding. He cannot think. His wife carried a pink purse, but no identification in it. He runs through the library, out the entrance, and stands at the top of the stairs. He scans the mass of people before him, and looks for a pink dress in a sea of muted blacks, browns and grays. At last he prays, "Oh, God, Oh God. Please, please, please…"

Dad races and stumbles down the stairs, then turns east on 42nd St. As he moves through the tide of swirling humanity, he starts to sob. "What do I tell my children? Please, God, please." After walking several more blocks he sees a flash of pink. He starts to run. A taxi honks and swerves to avoid him as he dashes across the street. Miraculously, not ten feet ahead, Mom is standing in front of a window gazing at the mannequins. He walks up to her and taps her shoulder. She smiles at him, as though nothing is wrong. "Let's go home," he says with a sigh. The faith that had eluded him since his wife's diagnosis returns. Looking up at the sky, a solitary tear slides down his face.

It was many years before Dad had the courage to tell us this story. He realized he made a profound error in judgement that day and did not want his children to judge him for it.

When we asked him why he did that, Dad just shrugged and said,"I didn't know what else to do."

My father was a proud, independent man who <u>never</u> asked anyone for help. His daily routine set the rhythm of his life. My mother's illness crumbled his world. Now he was in uncharted territory without a map or support. This was the mid 70's, long before Alzheimer's support groups existed. Families took care of their own. Dad felt strongly that it was his duty to take care of Mom; he didn't want to disrupt the lives of his children or friends.

For seven more years, Dad diligently cared for Mom. He bathed her, dressed her, and fed her. He took her for long walks, and drove her to his favorite places. I never heard him complain about a thing, not even when she needed diapers.

On the day my mother died, my father woke, looked at his wife sleeping peacefully beside him, put on his flannel robe and went to the kitchen to start breakfast. He returned to their bedroom to wake Mom. He turned her over, whispered her name and touched her gently. She did not wake. He hurried to my sister's room and shouted, "Something is wrong with Mom!"

My sister, a nurse, grabbed her stethoscope. She listened to Mom's heart, got up, then hugged our Dad. "She's gone."

I am a stronger person today because of my father. The patience, love and fortitude with which he cared for our mother during her long decline were nothing short of heroic. These lessons in unwavering and selfless devotion have been invaluable to me as I have navigated my own challenges. My father taught me, by example, that love grounds us. It gives our lives meaning and purpose. It is the beacon that lights our way.

Mom and Dad on their wedding day

ABOUT THE AUTHOR

I was born in Brooklyn and raised on Long Island as part of a large Italian-American family. After I graduated from Hofstra University with a dual major in English and Sociology, I worked as a Social Worker, often with the Cuban refugees.

In my mid thirties I moved with my family to Orange County, California where I worked in the medical field for twenty years and then seven years in Adult Education. Presently, I continue to teach yoga, the same class I have had for twenty-seven years.

My son and daughter both live nearby. My two grandsons, ages eight and nine, keep me constantly entertained with their views of the world.

My hobbies include reading, painting (watercolor and mixed media), and photography. In my youth and throughout college, I enjoyed writing poetry and songs but lost touch with that in my adulthood. This story is my first attempt at getting back into writing.

JANET RICE

I ALWAYS CALLED HIM UNKIE
by Lois W. Stern

Maurice Levenbron was my mother's youngest brother, entering World War II as a private, returning four years later as a captain. *Unkie* was stationed in the thick of battle in both North Africa and Italy during most of those years, facing heavy artillery, even leading the third battalion in the Battle at Monte Cassino. But he never dwelled on the hardships he faced, the tragedies he witnessed. By the time he returned to the US, his uniform was decorated with numerous bars and medals, but miraculously, none of them included a purple heart.

Maurice Levenbron, date unknown, wearing a 2nd lieutenant bar

I was a young child when he returned to the states, welcoming him with bear hugs, smothering him with kisses. But it didn't take long for me to toddle off to my bedroom, returning seconds later with a two foot tall stuffed panda bear that he had sent me from abroad. This panda was my constant companion. Although by then somewhat tattered from wear and tear, I dearly loved him. Somehow I suspect I innately felt the warmth and special affection emanating from the gift giver, this man I called *Unkie*.

A bachelor with no immediate ties, Unkie at first moved in with my parent, then married, built a home just a few miles distant from ours, where he and his wife raised their two daughters. Our families remained close, often dropping in unannounced and always welcome.

During those growing up years, there was rarely a quiet moment when he was in the room. He loved to chat and I loved to listen. When I learned about the days he and some of his battalion had been entrenched in a fox hole, I wanted to know more: "What was it like in there? Were you afraid? Did you see any of your comrades get killed?"

He was a great storyteller, but forever seemed to have that gift of focusing on the positive. He didn't answer those hard-to-recall events of the war, but instead chose to focus on the bright side: how he discovered an old rug sitting by the side of the road and dragged it into their hide out. My eyes opened wide as he recounted the incident with the words, "You'd be surprised how cozy we made it in there." And then there was the orphaned dog he found, wandering about hungry and emaciated, whom he adopted, named T-2 and made an honorary member of his battalion. But years later, while watching New York War Stories, a WLIW video, I suddenly saw him appear on the screen, recounting details of the day he led his battalion in the battle of Monte Casino, and stood by helplessly watching his wounded captain die a slow death. It was obvious he never forgot.

Unkie had a rare sense of humor. Easy going style, he could stretch out a story to five or six minutes that most of us would tell in a quarter of that time. Yet he managed to keep his audiences entranced, eyes focused and ears tuned to his every word. His smile and soft blue eyes were part of his charm, but there was something more, his ability to laugh at his own blunders. Things that most of us would like to bury from memory, cringing at the thought of sharing them with others, were rich fodder for his stories. One of my favorites was about the day he and his father were working on a carpentry project in their basement:

"Every few minutes my father was sending me upstairs to ask
my mother for another tool, but she was busy preparing a
company dinner and was losing patience with all the
interruptions. Finally, in her Yiddish tongue, she told me to tell
Papa, *Fah drai me nish ken cup* (Translation: "Tell Papa to stop
bothering me."). But when I delivered her message, my father
was so angry he didn't speak to her for days! Why? Although I
had done my best to translate her words from Yiddish to English,
the message I delivered was: "Mamma said, go bang your head
against a wall!"

Unkie, about age five

Before entering the war, *Unkie* had completed his college and graduate studies. He attended Lafayette College, a small yet well respected school overlooking the Delaware River in Easton, Pennsylvania, and made us laugh out loud when recounting an episode about his freshman year orientation.

"We sat in a large room and listened to some introductory remarks. Then we were each given a blue booklet and asked to write a short essay about a current events topic of our choice. Knowing my parents were waiting to take me into town to pick out an easy chair for my dorm room, all I could think of was, *I've got to get out of here.* I asked the proctor if this was a test, if it counted for anything, and being assured that it was of little consequence, I scratched out a few words post haste to join my parents for that shopping expedition. Two days later, I met with my advisor. After about fifteen minutes of congenial conversation, he looked me square in the eye and said, "You don't know how happy I am to meet you. When I read your essay, I was sure you were a moron, and thought to myself, *Oh, boy, this one's not going to last very long!*

But stay he did, graduating with honors and moving on to Fordham Law School in Manhattan, NY. As an attorney, he endeared himself to many of his clients. He was the old fashioned type attorney, who truly cared more about guiding each of his clients than charging big time, pay-per-hour fees. Never in a rush, fame and fortune were not what it was about for him.

Hired as general counsel to a large suburban school district, fifty years later they held a celebratory evening in recognition of his years of service. Many spoke laudatory words of his skills in resolving challenging issues, but they also chided him on how they eventually caught on to his game. When anticipating being presented with a particularly challenging legal issue, they noted how he would reach deep into his jacket pocket, pull out his pipe, slowly fill it with tobacco, sit back in his chair and take a few leisurely puffs - all accomplished in slow motion and utter silence. As the room filled with smoke, he would be weighing the options for the best resolution.

The years went by. His wife passed on, but he continued to be a joyful participant in his book group, golf outings and all our family gatherings. I felt a piece of me stolen when he moved to Laselle Village, an independent living facility situated on a college campus in Newton, Massachusetts. It was a good choice: He would be living close to his two daughters, and his new environment would continue to nurture his intellect and inquisitive mind, as residents were given a new course syllabus each semester and encouraged to register for their classes. How he loved those classes! I soon learned that if he was shut out of one that particularly interested him, he would seek out that professor and charm his way in!

Unkie, age 102

Unkie shut his eyes for the last time on December 2nd, 2018, at age 104. Several weeks before his demise, he sat discussing the book *Team of Rivals* with my husband and me and Brexit with our older son, Larry.

An indelible part of my life, his models of intellectual curiosity, generosity and humanity are constant reminders to me of the life I want to live. There are life lessons to be learned from Unkie's lifestyle. One can often find sheer joy in reaching out to help others, while retaining enough modesty to allow them to help us in return. Maurice Levenbron's way of life reminds me that inner satisfaction should be sufficient reward, without expectation of something tangible in return. As for his light hearted humor, his ability to dwell on the lilacs rather than the lemons of life, well, I'm still working on that one! But when I think of Unkie, I can't help but smile.

ABOUT THE AUTHOR

In 2012 I created *Tales2Inspire®*, this 'Authors Helping Authors' Project, which has gone viral, growing beyond my wildest expectations. I like to think of myself as both an author and author advocate. *Tales2Inspire* authors and I work as a team, fine tuning stories with high potential, until they are chiseled to perfection.

Many *Tales2Inspire* winners are seasoned authors whose stories require little to no editing, and of course I am thrilled when I receive stories already honed to perfection. But I am equally proud of those authors who have a beautiful story to share, but need to stay the course, edit, rewrite and edit some more, until their stories shine. We have become a community of well respected authors, and in many cases, long distance friends. I'm often asked why I spend so many. hours a day working on this project when I receive so little in return. (For if truth be known, based on the hours expended, I could probably earn more at a minimum wage job at MacDonalds!) But they are so wrong. This is a lesson I learned from Unkie, that inner satisfaction trumps money in the bank every time. Together we have now published ten *Tales2Inspire* books, and watching them come to life is a constant source of joy.

Lois W. Stern

TWINKLE, TWINKLE
by Wendy Russell-Sheppard

I sit in silence, regretting the promise. I have been brought to my knees, but force myself out of the car and into the dance studio for the first time.

Inside, I falter.

"There you are! Welcome, welcome! I'm Judy. Remember, we met at the party? I'm so happy to see you."

I can't help but notice. She walks with a slight limp. Her dazzling, rhinestone-studded buckles emphasize that one shoe is larger than the other.

I don't understand.

***

On this night, the ER is bathed in muted light. Assorted beeps and alarms punctuate the sombre ambiance. Under a warmed blanket, I am stunned. This cannot be happening. No smoking, no drinking. What did I do to deserve this? The IV drips like a water torture. The monitor is manic: a pulse rate of 158, an irregular, uncontrolled heart beat. It feels like a squirrel fight is ramping up in my chest. The treatment I receive makes it stop... for now.

The doctor explains. It has a name: atrial fibrillation. It barges in and takes over. There is no respite. A series of medications is ineffective. Debilitating side effects are the new normal.

Every task is an act of determination. I am a ticking time bomb. I could faint from wildly fluctuating blood pressure, or have a stroke, at any time. When I leave the house, I have no idea if I can get back. When I fall asleep, I have no idea when the next squirrel fight might jolt me awake. This generates waves of anxiety: more drugs, more side effects.

My devoted family and friends enfold me through years of emergencies.

Twinkle, Twinkle

On this morning, the ER is, once again, bathed in muted light. I block out the beeps and alarms. I decline the warmed blanket. My rage radiates like a blast furnace. Frustration boils up as I explain the lumps on my head. The meds have caused a loss of consciousness, a devastating fall. The ER doctor explains the concussion protocol. A neurosurgeon advises me about the three places in my brain that continue to bleed. This crisis resolves, but mind-numbing helplessness persists.

I used to feel powerful. Now I feel diminished.

My world used to feel limitless. Now, it shrivels to the size of the nest I build on the couch. I hunker down, exhausted, desperate to feel safe. I don't. My broken heart quivers within, a traitorous companion that I can't live without.

I descend into that wretched place I wanted to avoid- rock bottom. The walls of this prison are too slippery, the pit too deep. In the soul-searching hours before dawn, I study my pill bottles too closely, and contemplate the options.

Is this the rest of my life? What now? Is it time to give up?

With a desperate last gasp, I drag myself to a pot luck supper, and sense an unfamiliar energy. Judy's smile slices through my fog. Our eyes lock.

"You need to join my line dancing class. No experience necessary. I'll see you next Wednesday."

The idea is so preposterous, I stand there, mouth agape, silent.

"I'll see you next Wednesday."

She knows.

Week by week, dance by dance, a metamorphosis unfurls.

Judy becomes my touchstone, the voice I heed. "Okay, dancers, let's try this. We'll take it nice and slow, one step at a time. Oh, my hips are protesting. Never mind."

The music seeps into me. It is a blessed distraction. Something loosens.

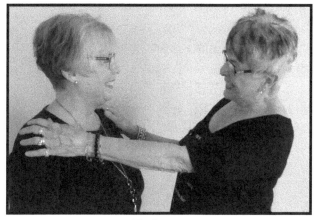

She knows

Judy nudges us along. "Flow with the music. Listen to your body. Take as many breaks as you need. Oops! Just a minute. I need to catch my breath."

There is unmistakable joy in Judy's love of dance, a selflessness in her efforts to share its regenerative powers.

She reminds us, "Don't be discouraged. It takes time. I can't dance the way I used to, but here I am. If my feet were the same size, I wouldn't stumble so often. Oh well."

Her support never waivers. Every person here is limping, but limping valiantly, toward acceptance of a chronic condition, embracing new limitations, filling new gaps with newer joy.

Judy takes us to her happy place. "This one is easy. You know all the steps. Focus on the 'twinkle'. Isn't that a lovely name for a dance step? One, two, three, one, two, three. Very nice, ladies. Looking good. Let's have some fun!"

I surrender to my new normal, and the remarkable happens. This is the only activity where I bat a thousand: not one heart problem, not ever. I clutch this kernel of consistency to my chest. My life depends on it.

Judy is nostalgic. "This is my father's favourite waltz. He was such a gentle soul. I think of him every time I hear it."

Judy's enthusiasm is contagious. She takes me out of myself and, with new-found wings, my heart soars.
"No matter what, just keep dancing!"
Now, I understand.

The Twinkle step

Slowly, very slowly, I feel a glimmer of hope. Slowly, very slowly, this glimmer ignites a blaze. Tenacity bubbles up from somewhere deep inside. It is time to take flight from my nest. Thanks to Judy, I now have the strength to do it.

Courage returns, and I confront my cardiologist.

I am too young for this.

This. Cannot. Be. The. Rest. Of. My. Life.

There has to be another option.

There is.

It seems like an eternity, but after several consultations at a heart institute, I undergo a procedure that eliminates my symptoms, and the need for medication. The crushing prospect of total incapacitation fades into the background. I resume my normal activities, a little more slowly, a little less often. I make peace with my newly-refurbished companion.

I am re-energized in my search for new adventures, thanks to a dazzling, rhinestone-studded role model. Judy has taught me to persevere, to pursue new passions, even in the shadow of chronic illness. She has shown me the way, one twinkle at a time.

***

The phone rings. It is the last person I expect.

"Hi. It's Judy. I hate to bother you, but I need your help. My husband has just been diagnosed with atrial fibrillation. He feels terrible and doesn't know what to do. The meds aren't working. He's tired all the time. He can't think straight. He's getting pretty discouraged. He really needs to talk to somebody. Would you mind if he called you?"

I am familiar with the desperation in her voice. In a heartbeat, she has my answer.

It is my turn to lead, and we will keep dancing, until this melody fades to silence.

My turn to lead

ABOUT THE AUTHOR

Wendy Russell-Sheppard is emerging from her comfortable chrysalis of academic writing into the exhilarating world of creative nonfiction. She is inspired by members of a Writers Helping Writers Group in Belleville, Ontario, as well as the Sarasota Writers' Group in Florida. Her husband is a loyal cheerleader. Wendy has a Bachelor of Arts Degree and a Master of Education Degree. She is an experienced mother, teacher, property renovator, general contractor and race car driver.

WENDY RUSSELL-SHEPPARD

A LEGACY OF STRENGTH
In loving memory of Mama and Papa
by Jane Forgey

With these words, my husband announced he was leaving us. "Get yourself a lawyer. I want a divorce!" For years I had worked endless hours in our forty-five-seat coffee shop, Muffin Korner, trying to hold our lives together. I thought I was doing everything possible to help. I was in shock. No one in my family had ever gotten a divorce. Having no self-confidence, and never having plans or goals of my own, I knew in an instant I was in the deepest trouble of my life.

I am paralyzed with fear. I tell my children, "I cannot explain what has happened, or your father's actions." I have no answers to their tearful and heart wrenching questions. Why did he leave us? Doesn't he love us? When is Daddy coming home? My teenage daughters, ages fourteen and sixteen, and my son, age eighteen, cannot begin to fathom something like this could ever happen to our family. Each one withdraws into their own separate space, terrified. I feel distraught for everyone. All I can say is, "Don't get into any trouble. Don't make my life more difficult. Please, stay clear of bad influences and drugs." They roll their eyes until they realize we are down and out, abandoned. Daddy is not coming home, not even for them. I cannot utter one sentence without cursing. My children look at me frightened, and tremble at my irate voice. Every night afraid, I cry.

I am now my family's only breadwinner, a situation I never thought would occur. Constantly apprehensive about my children's mental health and attitudes, I scrutinize their sullen faces. I worry about the bills, the house mortgage, the shop's rent, repairs, my business, and the competition. I am traumatized and overwhelmed. I do not know what to do. Should I sell the business? How will I support us? How will we survive? These questions continuously plague my mind. I need a plan.

Not feeling educated or smart, feeling irresponsible and depressed, I sought the guidance of a psychologist. Because she was compassionate, I was able to tell her how unimportant and inconsequential I felt. As the last of eight children, and a twin, I only saw myself as my twin sister's shadow. I felt invisible, never giving myself credit for the value of my thoughts. Over time my therapist helped me realize my resourcefulness. "Has anything really changed?" she asked. After all, I had always worked the shop on my own. She advised me to stop wasting my energy on the past and to look to the future. It was then that I understood. While running the shop, I had emerged as a real person, my own person, capable and confident.

During my divorce, I began to think about how my parents managed the difficulties of their lives. I realized just how much I had learned from their example. After my father's military service in WWI, my parents were married and emigrated from Sicily through Ellis Island. They settled in New York City. It was 1920. They were only twenty-five and eighteen.

Mama and Papa holding twins

They often spoke of how harrowing it was to leave their families and friends behind. however they recognized that there was no opportunity for them in their war-ravaged country. They are equipped with only elementary educations and aspirations for a better life. They were brave and resilient, both finding jobs, my father as a dock worker and my mother as a seamstress, raising six children through the depression.

When Papa was fifty and Mama forty-three, they welcomed my twin sister and me into the family. With hard work and dedication to each other, they raised eight good children by demanding that we be truthful, obey the family's rules, the laws of the land, and the priority, graduate from high school and get a job. I remember my father's strong warning. "Stay on the straight road," meaning stay out of trouble.

The counselor advised me to make my children take on more responsibility. She said, "Do not allow them to blame you for no clean laundry, no home cooked meals." They could not comprehend we had no money as I counted each day's receipts.

In small steady increments, my plan became clear. I must keep the business I had established. I must remain vigilant raising my teenagers. They must remain responsible … Remembering Papa's words, I repeated them over and over. "You only have me to call. Stay out of trouble."

Being a tough mother, keeping my children on a constructive path was more difficult than all the other jobs I had ever had. I told them, "You must graduate high school. You will go to college. Learn from my mistakes. You must equip yourselves with options. Do not be ill prepared for your future!"

On occasion, my children had accompanied me to Muffin Korner. Now, I required them to work weekends, holidays, and during their summer vacations, keeping the money within our household. Child-support and alimony were unreliable. As teenagers, of course they were unwilling, grumbling, "Why do we have to work? What about our schoolwork? And our friends?" They felt trapped with me. "Ok," I said, "Get another job!"

They took minimum wage jobs, but decided it was more advantageous to work with me. I was flexible with their schedules and compensated them as they, too, learned to do short order cooking, meal preparation, waitressing, cleaning, public relations, human resourcing, purchasing, and whatever else was required at the shop. As their skills grew, I increased their wages. They could see the rewards of working hard and how far the money did not go.

Jane and Daughter – Working together to make it work

Needing money for mounting college expenses, I extended our hours to accommodate the influx of summer visitors, cottage people, and boaters that inundated our coastal town. Normally, we closed at 1 PM, but now we opened for dinner as well. On Fridays and Saturdays, we remained open all night accommodating the "After the Bar" crowd. I worked the night shift while my teenagers handled the day and evening hours.

Jane and daughters – A Legacy of Strength

Muffin Korner sustained us. I remained at the shop for twelve years after my divorce. When I sold my business, I held my head high. I felt proud of my Muffin Korner, and my life. I felt loved and admired by all. Our hard work paid off. It was good for the soul of my family as well as the community.

As I reflect on the lives of my children, I feel deeply saddened by the loss of their carefree childhood, no longer laughing or having spontaneous fun. Everyday pressures burdened them as they hung on to the hope a call would come and their drastically changed lives would return to normal. However, it was beyond my control. I told them, "Stay strong," as I remembered Mama's words to me.

I would not have survived without my children. I am thankful and proud of them. Experiencing the pitfalls and perils of life helped them to see the importance of achieving goals. They realized hard work enhanced their self-esteem, and integrity. One daughter is now a dental hygienist and the other is a teacher. My son is a successful engineer. They are happily married with families of their own.

I also reflect upon the lives of my parents. Starting their lives over in a new country required true grit. My husband walked out on us, which forced me to start my life over as well.

My parents' example was a reliable standard, one I could fall back on time and again, as my children and I were forced to discover our own inner strengths.

My family is stronger today. Pulling together to survive our many challenges helped all of us to become wise and self-assured. It made us the empowered individuals we are today.

ABOUT THE AUTHOR

I have excelled in life because of perseverance. My life has taken many turns and afforded me many opportunities. I take a nothing ventured, nothing gained attitude.
I have experienced life as a travel agent, entrepreneur, and life coach to my children and young employees. I also loved being the pre-nursery school Nanny for my six grandchildren.
As a new writer I benefit from reading and crafting my own stories, with the help of shared knowledge of other writers. I enjoy the satisfaction and accomplishment of a story well done.
Born and raised in New York, I enjoy life in Connecticut and Florida with my husband Don.

JANE FORGEY

MISS DeYOUNG
by Adrienne Drake, MD

The trauma of my seventh year remains with me even today. Yet, along with those harsh memories come fond thoughts of my third-grade teacher. When I was seven years old, my parents went through a bitter and lengthy divorce. My slightly older brother and I had front row seats to the hostilities, and were spared none of the fallout.

When the time came for us to leave our home, my mother hastily packed my brother, me and our turquoise parakeet, Piper, into the backseat of her 1950's blue Ford, aptly named "The Battle Axe." When I asked her why Piper was along for this particular ride she curtly explained, "Your father doesn't love you anymore, so we are going to move to a new house."

In those days, there was no freeway between Los Angeles and Seal Beach and the thirty-mile ride seemed endless. Piper complained, and so did my brother, but true to form, I remained quiet as could be, huddled in the back seat of The Battle Axe. I wondered what I had done to cause this disruption in our lives, worried that I might never see my father again, pondered what I had done to make him stop loving us, and asked myself how I could ever right this terrible wrong.

The first day in my new third-grade class was a nightmare. Although my mother had chosen Seal Beach because "the school system was so much better," a fringe benefit for her was that we now lived only a few miles away from Long Beach, where an old college sweetheart, with whom she had rekindled a relationship, now lived.

The new school *was* much better than the school I had left. In Los Angeles, I was just learning math using ice cream sticks as counters. Here, they were already learning Roman numerals. School had always been my refuge, but now, I was as lost in school as I was in life. Soon my teacher, Miss DeYoung, noticed my distress. She spent every lunch hour with me until

105

I knew the meaning of I, V, X, L , C and M, and how to use them to make numbers I could deal with.

In her class, you could earn extra credit points by doing additional homework pages. Already an overachiever, I grabbed at the opportunity to gain all the extra credit I could, and therefore garner praise and recognition, and most importantly, self-esteem. I told myself I would have the most points by the end of the year. I had to win that prize. I forfeited my lunch hours to do the additional work.

Miss DeYoung took note. "Don't you want to go out and play with your new friends?" she would gently inquire. I will never forget the concern in her voice, or the kind way she looked directly into my sad eyes with her sparkling hazel green ones. But, I always stayed inside, now as much to absorb her softness as to earn the extra points.

Adrienne, age 8

As the weeks went on, Miss DeYoung and I offered each other a certain kind of company. The very nearness of her was the most attention I had ever received. She never went outside either, and in that way, I felt we were kindred spirits. I knew better than to stare. Nonetheless, I always loved to look at her while she bent over her desk eating lunch. While I wolfed down my PB and J's, I wondered what could be in her *green* sandwiches. I marveled at the way she wore her long brown hair in a neat French roll, or a tidy bun, so natural and different from my mother's close-cropped fake platinum blonde, which always creeped me out. While my mother smelled like alcohol and cigarettes, Miss DeYoung smelled like fresh roses. She became a quiet, stable presence in my life.

One day, I asked her what made her sandwiches green. "Oh. It's avocado. Have you ever eaten an avocado before?" My mother wasn't much into cooking, so there was a lot about food I didn't know. And I had never even seen an avocado. I am sure Miss DeYoung had noticed the quality of my lunches as well, and from that day forward, she always brought me an extra half sandwich, made of avocado. It was the best thing I had ever tasted.

One lunch period, Miss DeYoung brought me some paper dolls. I had actually never seen a paper doll and was intrigued. "You can buy one of these dolls with your extra credit points," she told me with a smile. Although I had started this third grade class two months into the school year, after six months, I had more extra credit points than anyone else, but only by a slim margin. And I really wanted my own paper doll. Knowing this would put me behind in credits, still, I could not resist purchasing the adorable drum majorette with the long lanky legs. I imagined her in a navy drummer costume with all of its stripes and buttons. She cost me dearly: twenty-five hard-earned points. For the rest of the week, I colored her outfits with crayons and pieced her appendages to her torso with little brass fasteners. For her baton, I glued a white paper drinking straw to her left hand and curled her white gloved fingers around it.

By the end of the academic year, with the help of Miss DeYoung and our lunch hours together, I had regained my academic confidence. She became a refuge from my unstable, unhappy mother. When it came time to hand out the award for the student with the most extra credits earned, I came in second.

But by now, that "extra credit" prize no longer mattered to me. The lessons I learned from Miss DeYoung went far beyond those of, "Always do your best to be your best." She offered a lonely, lost child, patience, and kindness. Her actions let me know without a doubt that I mattered. She encouraged me to be playful. She taught me that a life out of control does not always need to be managed with control, self-depravation and awards. She was a bridge for me from chaos to compassion.

To this day, I love avocados. I never eat one without saying a silent prayer of thanks for my dear third grade teacher. I smile at the memories as I ask myself, "Will I ever forget the lessons that she taught me?" The answer is always, "Never."

I was so fortunate to have Miss DeYoung in my life. I wish I could tell her today what she meant to me. I am seventy now, and it is too late. I was seven then, and I was too young to appreciate the value of her authentic caring. Now, I recognize that she came into my life exactly when I needed her. At a very traumatic time of my childhood, her consistent tenderness and love empowered me. She gave me the confidence I needed to believe in myself. She was one of many angels along the way who saved me.

ABOUT THE AUTHOR

My job as a physician practicing Internal Medicine and
Infectious Diseases required careful observation, detailed
questioning, and much reflection upon what my patients told me.
When someone was in my office for a routine examination, I had
the luxury of time. I could ask them about their lives. I loved to
learn about their families, goals and dreams. However, when I
was seeing a patient with an acute illness, I had to be much more
focused in order to elicit the hidden clues that would help lead
me to a correct diagnosis. My written records of these sacred
encounters were referred to, in medical jargon, as the patient's
"History." They were, in fact, *their stories.*
Now that I am retired, I continue to observe my surroundings and
to ask myself questions. In this way, I try to make sense of my
life and of the world around me. And then, I write. These written
reflections are *my stories*. I hope that you will enjoy them.

ADRIENNE DRAKE, MD

A Letter to My Readers

Dear Reader,

Once I learned that the Opal is a karmic stone, meaning that what we put out comes back to us, I knew it would be the perfect gem to represent this collection of stories. From the Greek derivative "Opallios", meaning *to see a change of color*, the opal is absorbent and reflective, helping us pick up thoughts and feelings, amplify them and return them to their place of origin. What a perfect fit for a collection of Stronger Today . .. stories, true stories each author tells of a person or event that impacted them deeply, in some cases changing the trajectory of their lives.

After each new *Tales2Inspire* collection is published, I'm often asked, "Which book is your favorite?" The truth is, I think I fall in love with most every story that finds its way into one of these collections. But I really would like to know which ones are your favorites.

If you have read this book, appreciate the skill of these authors and have felt the power of their stories, please help give them the recognition they deserve by writing a review highlighting the stories that particularly resonated with you. You see, reviews can be tough to come by these days, but readers rely on them to make decisions about the books they buy. You, the reader, now have the power to make or break a book, so it would be so awesome if you would take the time to write a review and post it on Amazon.com (and any other cool places you can think of.)

And because I like to express my appreciation to those who help us, if you send an e-mail once your review is posted, I have a special surprise for you!

E-mail: tales2inspire@optimum.net

Lois W. Stern

NOTE: If you're not sure what to include in a review and need some inspiration, check out the book club discussion questions on the next several pages to spark your own creativity.

BOOK CLUB DISCUSSION QUESTIONS
Spark Your Creativity

1. *Gayla, Lost in Pink* and *Twinkle, Twinkle* are three stories in this collection focused on people either directly or indirectly dealing with a serious illness. What do these stories suggest to you about facing some of these more difficult life challenges?

2. At first glance the subjects of the two stories, *Eugene* and *I Always Called Him Unkie,* seem like very different men. Yet despite their differences, what traits do they share in common? What inspirations can you glean from some of their basic human characteristics to pass along to others?

3. Sometimes we have to step back from the frantic pace of our lives to transcend from utter chaos to tranquility. How does the story, *The Swan,* gives us that perspective about mother nature's helping hand?

4. It is not surprising that several of the Stronger Today stories focus on the impact of an educator on the life of a child. Which of these stories touched you most deeply and why? Can you relate to any of these children's experiences?

5. *Triumph Over Trauma, What is Life?* and *Legacy of Strength* are stories of survival after traumatic experiences. What do these stories tell you about the strength of the human spirit?

6. *The Swan* and *Mr. Hoots* are fine examples of the power of mother nature. What inspired you most about either of these stories.

7. Why do you think the Opal is a good choice as the gemstone to represent this particular collection of stories?

Ready to write a review?
Just copy:

https://www.amazon.com/s?
k=Tales2Inspire+Collection&i=stripbooks&qid=1446640172&ref=sr_gnr_fk
mr1

into your browser.
And I thank you ever so much!

Lois W. Stern

113

Gifts and Special Offers

Tales2Inspire ~The Emerald Collection
DO YOU BELIEVE IN COINCIDENCES?

This book is filled with contest winning tales that feature those special encounters that may or may not be accidental. One tale after another will make you believe that life is more than just a series of chance meetings.

A girl learns that her childhood heroine is actually her biological sister. They meet and discover that their handwriting, talents and interests are exactly the same. . . . A runaway dog sits in a garden miles from home, too frightened to move. Its frantic owner stops a total stranger, who turns out to be the one person who can lead her to her dog. These and more *Beyond Coincidence* award-winning stories will make you wonder if we are really as free as we think we are, or if there are unknown forces guiding our lives.

The **Emerald,** the symbol for intuitive awareness, is the perfect gemstone to symbolize this collection of beyond coincidence stories.

Tales for the Heart and Soul
Is it true that there are no coincidences in life? If you believe as I do that there is an energy that goes beyond the five senses, then this book is a must read for you. The Emerald Collection is the perfect subtitle for the beautifully crafted gems that are yours to read over and over again.
Glenn Poveromo, Motivational teacher
Author of *The Power of Visualization, Change Your Thinking Change Your Life, The Spirits Self-Help Book, Learn to Live Your Best Life Ever*

Tales2Inspire ~The Topaz Collection

WHAT STORIES BRING US PERSONAL AWAKENINGS?

Stories of mind jolting, eye opening experiences that have changed the lives of these authors evermore.

From famous district attorney, Maurice Nadjari's *All that Glitters*; and Sharon Johnson's *God Must Have Wanted Me to Smile*, to multi-award-winning author, Mark H. Newhouse's poignant story of how he lost his family's history, and many more, you won't be able to stop reading.

The Topaz: The symbol for self-realization and confidence, brings us a collection of *Personal Awakenings* stories.

Powerful Lessons in Perspective

Though my goal with the book was entertainment, many of the stories teach powerful lessons . . . There were lines that stopped me in my tracks. . . , a high achieving diabetic admonishing his over-protective mother with, *Mom, do you own this disease or do I?;* an adopted girl's realization about true happiness, the incredible bond between a Dr. and her 7- year quadriplegic patient. . . an enjoyable and enlightening book.

John Graden
Author and journalist
Near Death Experiences-Doctors and Scientists Go On The Record About God, Heaven, and the Afterlife"

Tales2Inspire ~The Sapphire Collection

WHAT STORIES ECHO IN OUR MIND LONG AFTER WE'VE READ THEM?

Spell-binding stories of timeless memories you'll want to shout about and pass along to your family and friends. From famous district attorney, Maurice Nadjari's *All that Glitters*; and Sharon Johnson's *God Must Have Wanted Me to Smile*, to multi-award-winning author, Mark H. Newhouse's poignant story of how he lost his family's history, and many more, you won't be able to stop reading.

The Sapphire, the symbol for communication, insight and inspiration, brings us a collection of *Timeless Memories* to echo in your mind.

A young boy plans a wonderful surprise for his pappy - an opportunity to join some circus band musicians for an afternoon of tooting. Later he learns that he gave his pappy the most special day of his life. A teacher uses her dog to help manage her class of special needs students. A boy with severe behavior problems stops acting out, at first whispering secrets in the dog's ear, later making friends within his class. We hope these award winning stories inspire you, the reader, to recall some of your timeless memories, too precious to be forgotten, to inspire you, your family and friends.

Memorable Threads in the Fabric of Life
The writing . . . has been painstakingly chiseled to near perfection, with each story accompanied by one or more photographs. . . . The text has been put together with care and artistry, making it a truly pleasurable read.
Bani Sodermark
Amazon Vine Voice Reviewer
Official reviewer for *Book Pleasures*

Tales2Inspire ~The Ruby Collection

WHAT PRECIOUS GIFT CAN WE GIVE TO OTHERS WITHOUT SPENDING A DIME?

Of course, it's the *Gifts of Compassion*. From Melanie Sue Bowles' story of how she rescues and nurtures an abused, emaciated horse, to John Graden's story of the black belt champion who fights to keep ghetto children out of harm's way, this collection of award-winning stories might just inspire you to live your life with a more open heart.

The Ruby, the symbol for friendship and love, was carefully selected to represent this particular collection of gift of compassion stories.

A Whopping TEN
On a scale of 1 to 5, *Tales2Inspire ~ The Ruby Collection* is a whopping TEN! When you think times are tough for you, then you need to read this particular book. It will inspire you to never give up. The courage that these people show is unbelievable. Now go out and buy all the books in the *Tales2Inspire* collection.
Michael Monji
Amazon Vine Voice reviewer

Tales2Inspire ~The Garnet Collection

WHAT CAN WE HUMANS LEARN FROM ANIMALS?

You will read some amazing stories of animals covered in either feathers or fur. Read Audrey Stone's story of how her service dog stood between her and a minibus, to protect her from the brunt of its impact. Dayle Finn tells the amazing story of a white goose who befriends a near blind lab, taking him on daily walks while serving as his 'guide dog'. These and more of the award-winning stories in this collection share tales of some incredible animals and the burst of energy they give the humans who love them.

The Garnet was well chosen as the symbol for this collection, as it is known to revitalize and boost energy, just as our animal friends do for us.

Animals and Miracles
We have so much to learn from animals, their lives and their behavior, for they are complete while man is not. This book of heartwarming animal stories can continue to teach and help us all.
Dr. Bernie Siegel
Author of *Love, Animals and Miracles, 365 Prescriptions for the Soul,* and *A Book of Miracles*

Tales2Inspire ~The Crystal Collection

WHAT TYPE STORIES ARE LIKELY TO TICKLE THE FUNNY BONE?

You will laugh at the failed experience of the brash young man who takes his girlfriend for a sail, but by the end of the day, has lost both boat and girlfriend. We giggle with amusement at the musical valentine that has a hidden Sonny and Cher surprise under its heart shaped cover. In the words of Josh Billings, *Laughter is the sensation of feeling good all over and showing it principally in one place.* The award-winning stories in this collection help us feel good all over, bringing a smile to our lips and some joy to our hearts.

The Crystal, like humor, is known for its healing properties, for it lifts our spirits, transporting us from the here and now to several moments of pure amusement.

Official Apex 5-Star review

. . . a thoroughly humorous collection of short stories, The Crystal Collection highlights a plethora of different emotions and experiences, spreading their humor in indiscriminate fashion. From youthful attempts at avoiding punishment to the verity of being a redhead - to yes, even a chicken zombie - The Crystal Collection is sure to open readers' eyes to, and help boost their appreciation of, the lighter side of life.

Highly recommended.

Monique Franklin, Apex Reviews

Author, playwright, frequent blogger as The Alaska Philosophaster,

Tales2Inspire ~The Pearl Collection

WHAT ARE OUR KIDS UP TO THESE DAYS?

You will be amazed at the some of the awesome things these kids are doing to better our world! From saving gorillas slated for black market poaching, to rescuing dogs from kill shelters, from supplying needy children with backpacks filled with school supplies, to activists working to clean up our environment..... Feeling discouraged about the next generation? Read their stories for a burst of optimism.

The Pearl: the symbol for youth, purity and generosity, is the perfect match for the stories that fill the pages of this book. You are about to meet some awesome kids, kids making an incredible impact to better our world.

If I could give this book 6 stars, I would.
If you want to be inspired about our future on this planet, and if you need some perking up about the condition of the next generation, please read this incredible book. You will be well-rewarded when you read the real life stories of these young people who are sincerely making a positive difference in our world.
Terry Atkinson
South African author of *A Love Story from the Heart*" and *Bob and the Bully*.

ACKNOWLEDGEMENTS

Special thanks to:

Jessica Stern for her special insights and artistic vision in creating the cover for this book.
Graphic Artist
jessicaestern24@gmail.com

Sean Somics who created the logo which appears in the center of the cover of each *Tales2Inspire* anthology.
Graphic Artist
805.451.8794b

Our talented editors:
Rod DiGruttolo
rodshs62@hotmail.com
&
Adrienne Drake, M.D.
art4aad@aol.com

To all the *Tales2Inspire* authors whose stories are published in this book, you are an awesome group of writers and friends.